MODELLING
AND
FLAT CUTTING
FOR
FASHION

3

by the same author

Modelling and Flat Cutting for Fashion 1
Modelling and Flat Cutting for Fashion 2

MODELLING
AND
FLAT CUTTING
FOR
FASHION

3

Helen Stanley, ACFI, MSIAD

Senior Lecturer in Clothing,
London College of Fashion

HUTCHINSON

London   Melbourne   Sydney   Auckland   Johannesburg

Hutchinson & Co. (Publishers) Ltd

An imprint of the Hutchinson Publishing Group

17–21 Conway Street, London W1P 6JD

Hutchinson Group (Australia) Pty Ltd
30–32 Cremorne Street, Richmond South, Victoria 3121
PO Box 151, Broadway, New South Wales 2007

Hutchinson Group (NZ) Ltd
32–34 View Road, PO Box 40–086, Glenfield, Auckland 10

Hutchinson Group (SA) (Pty) Ltd
PO Box 337, Bergvlei 2012, South Africa

First published 1982

Designed and typeset by DP Press, Sevenoaks, Kent

Printed in Great Britain by The Anchor Press Ltd
and bound by Wm Brendon & Son Ltd
both of Tiptree, Essex

British Library Cataloguing in Publication Data
Stanley, Helen
    Modelling and flat cutting for fashion.
    3
    1. Dressmaking – Pattern design
    I. Title
    646.4'3204   TT520

ISBN 0 09 147490 6 cased
      0 09 147491 4 paper

Contents

To my students, past and present

Preface

As with *Modelling and Flat Cutting for Fashion 1 and 2*, this book is also concerned with imparting basic skills and knowledge to designers and pattern cutters to translate their design ideas and working sketches into accurate garment patterns.

The programme of work employs both modelling and flat pattern cutting methods and is presented in the form of self-contained 'lessons' with text and diagrams closely related. This feature has proved advantageous to lecturers and teachers when preparing course and lesson material; to students of dress and fashion following BA and MA degree courses, college diplomas, TEC or DATEC diplomas, CGLI and O- and A-level examination courses; to pattern cutters and designers working on their own, in the theatre and television, or in industry; and to many lay designers and home dressmakers.

Metric measurements, with imperial values in brackets, are used throughout the book to facilitate the change to the metric system.

I should like to thank Mr E. D. Wade, MA, BSc (Econ.), ACIS, MBIM, principal of the London College of Fashion, for allowing me to use the college facilities; Mrs M. Ross, BA, ALA, chief librarian, Mrs B. Smith, BA, ALA, and Miss D. Prewett, BA, ALA, assistant librarians, for their assistance during research; and my students, for trying out and proving the accuracy of the modelling and flat pattern cutting exercises.

My acknowledgements and grateful thanks are due to Winant, Towers Limited, who kindly gave me permission to reproduce the illustrations on pages 46 and 56 from *English Women's Clothing in the Present Century*, C. Willett Cunnington (Faber & Faber 1956).

I am especially grateful to Doug Fox, Anne Howes and Eric Drewery, for their invaluable advice and guidance during the preparation for press.

Finally, I would like to thank Walter, John and Edward Stanley for their patience and understanding.

Helen Stanley
1982

Introduction

The large quantity of styles produced in the fashion industry, influenced by sociological, ethnic and ergonomic factors, demands from today's designer and pattern cutter a greater degree of versatility to apply his knowledge to more than one facet of fashion. For example, he must be able to produce patterns for jackets, jeans, shorts and panties, jodhpur breeches, jumpsuits, and trousers in general; be able to develop patterns for maternity dresses and separates, as well as being skilful in the styling of day-to-day fashion clothes. This book, therefore, has been written to satisfy this need. The styles and fashion features are essential additional material to *Modelling and Flat Cutting for Fashion 1 and 2*.

Important styles, such as cascade drapery in wrapover skirts, raglan and two-piece sleeves are not shown in isolation but are incorporated and developed in the chapters on maternity wear and jacket block development. These styles can, of course, be extracted by the reader and used in the design of other garments. A glance at the index will help to select immediately the item that is required.

Figure 1

Figure 2

Figure 3

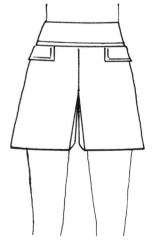

Figure 4

9

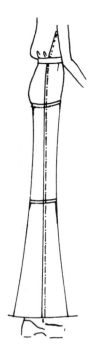

Figure 5

The work is presented with the three-dimensional approach of a sculptor to his creation, employing one or more methods of combining modelling with flat pattern cutting, working directly on the dress form and the human figure in a suitable trial fabric and, on occasions, in paper. In the case of maternity wear, the dress form is padded to the required dimensions before the toile and final pattern is developed. Sections of the garments are draped, adjusted and pinned until the desired effect and silhouette is achieved. This method enables designers to note at once the proportions of seam lines and dart positions and ascertain the position and relationship of pockets, buttons and buckles to design and fabric. Stripes, checks and other prominent patterns on fabrics can be indicated in pencil on the modelling material and trimmings can be assessed and moved around until the designer is satisfied with the 'final look'. This is an easy method which leads to quick and accurate results and appeals to the artistic and visually-orientated person; it does not involve intricate calculations.

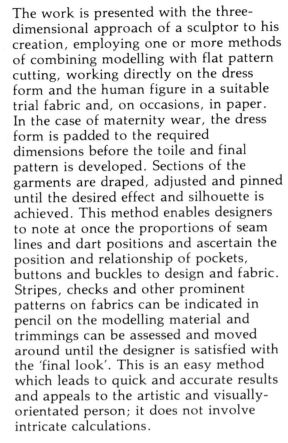

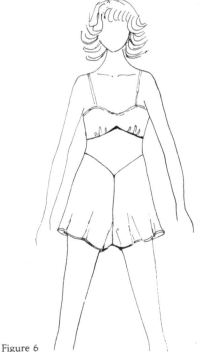

Figure 6

Figure 7

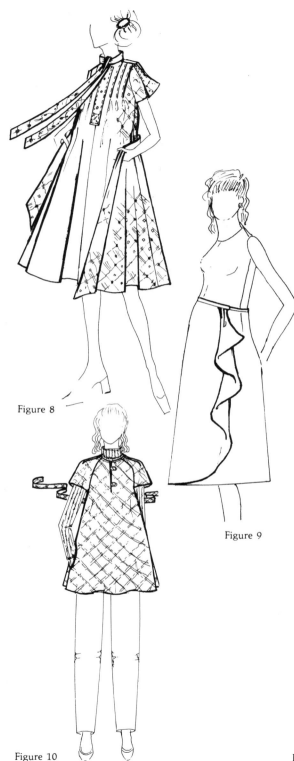

Readers are advised to observe current fashion trends, take note of the prevailing fashion silhouettes by looking at fashionable garments displayed in boutiques and fashion stores and to study fashion literature. Ideally, the designer should work on a dress form that incorporates the very latest fashion silhouette. Failing this, a fashionable silhouette can be obtained by making small adjustments to the dress form, for example, moving seam lines or padding the dress form and then modelling the trial garment accordingly. New lines, representing the silhouette, are then transferred to the basic blocks for further use.

Fifth scale block patterns are given at the beginning of this book on pages 12–15. These are helpful for purposes of experimentation and subsequent use by students in compiling personal reference folders.

Basic techniques for the development of basic patterns are covered in detail in *Modelling and Flat Cutting for Fashion 1*, and briefly in *Book 2*. Both books contain modelling techniques and detailed pattern developments for a wide variety of styles.

Figure 8

Figure 9

Figure 10

Figure 11

$\frac{1}{5}$ Scale Blocks Size 12

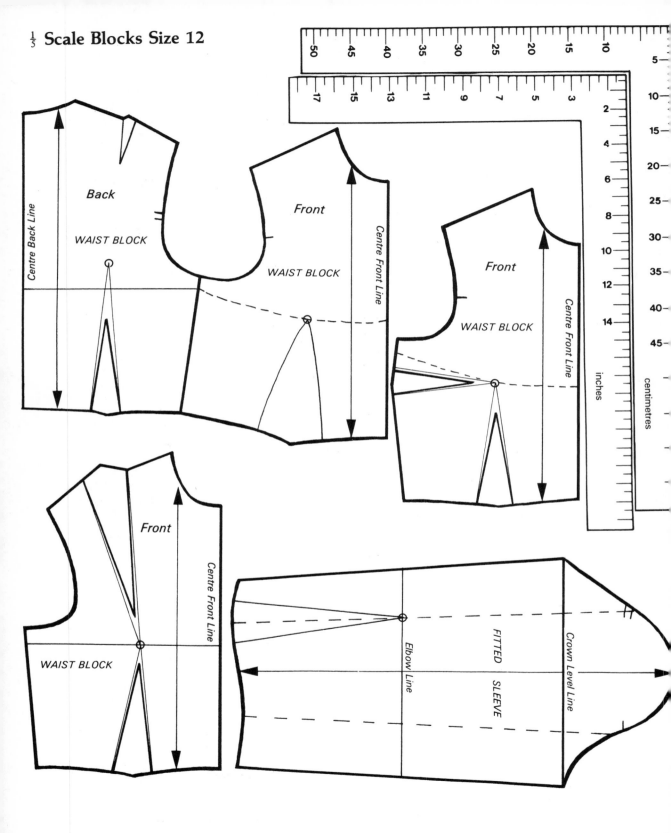

$\frac{1}{5}$ Scale Blocks Size 12

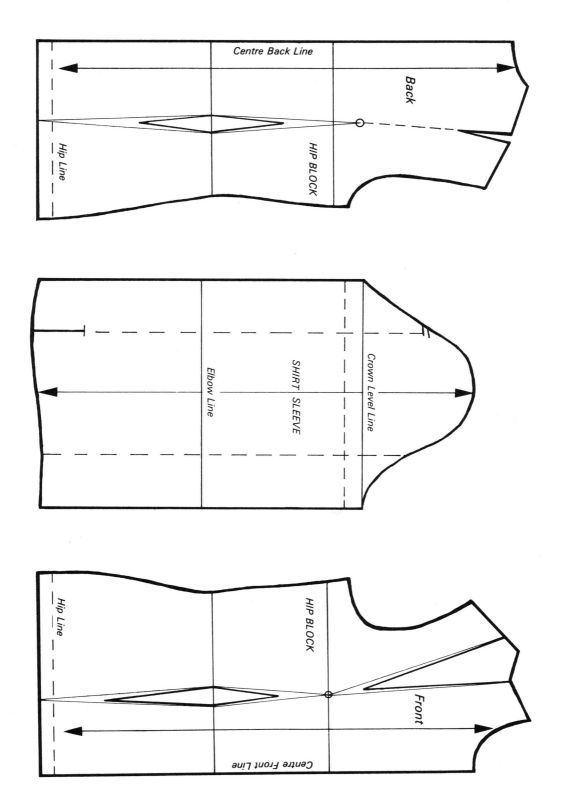

13

$\frac{1}{5}$ Scale Blocks Size 12

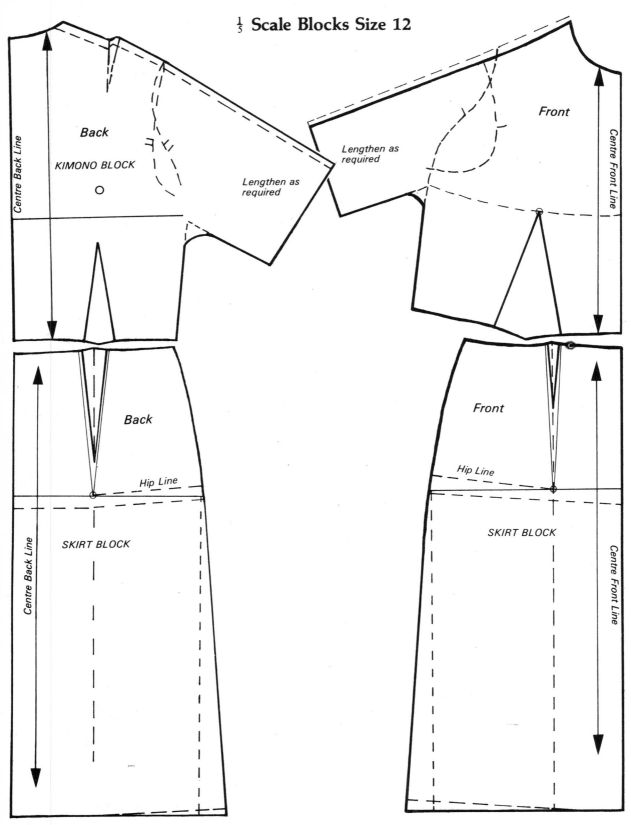

Back

KIMONO BLOCK

Centre Back Line

Lengthen as required

Lengthen as required

Front

Centre Front Line

Back

Hip Line

SKIRT BLOCK

Centre Back Line

Front

Hip Line

SKIRT BLOCK

Centre Front Line

$\frac{1}{5}$ Scale Blocks Size 12

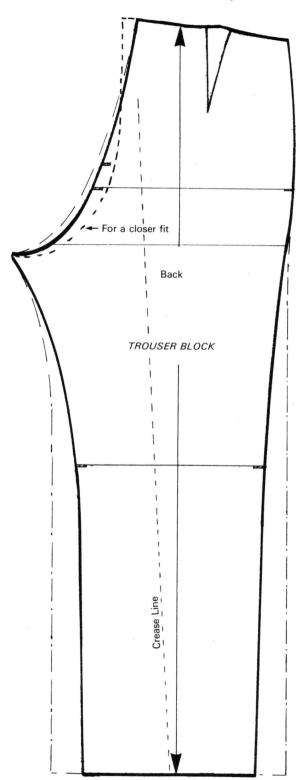

For a closer fit

Back

TROUSER BLOCK

Crease Line

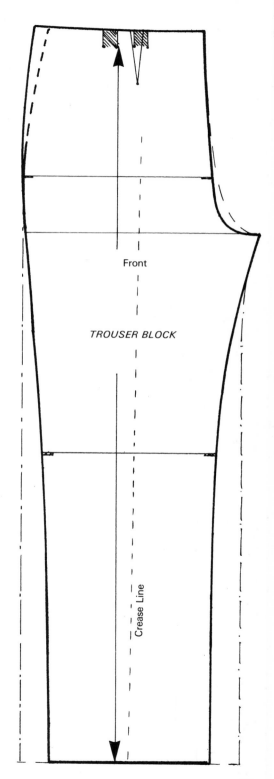

Front

TROUSER BLOCK

Crease Line

Metric size chart

Based on the average figure of average height of 164–169 cm

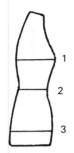

Size	36	38	40	42	44
To fit	10	12	14	16	18
Bust	82	87	92	97	102
Hips	87	92	97	102	107

Finished measurements

	36	38	40	42	44
1 Bust	92	97	102	107	112
2 Waist	65	70	75	80	85
3 Hips (20 cm down from waist)	97	102	107	112	117

Front and arm measurement

	36	38	40	42	44
1 Neck girth	35.5	36.5	37.5	38.5	39.5
2 Across chest (10 cm from pit of neck)	34	35	36	37.5	39
3 Armhole circumference	41	42	43	44	45.5
4 Upper arm girth	32	33	34	35.5	37
5 Wrist	19.5	20.5	21.5	22.5	23.5
6 Sleeve length	58	58.5	59	59.5	59.5

Back measurements, length and trouser measurements

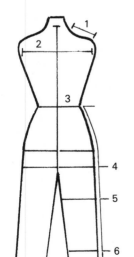

	36	38	40	42	44
1 Shoulder length	12.5	13	13.5	13.5	14
2 Across back (10 cm from nape)	35.5	36.5	37.5	39	40.5
3 Nape to waist	39	40	41	41.5	42
4 Body rise from waist	25.5	26	26.5	27	28
5 Thigh level (half hip to knee) approximately 39 cm from waist					
5 Thigh girth (according to style) from 55–63 cm					
6 Knee level 56–61 cm from waist					
6 Knee girth (according to style) 40–49–60 cm					
7 Outside leg (according to height) 100 cm plus from waist					
8 Trouser bottom width (according to style) 32–44–60 cm					

Seam allowances

1.5 to 2.5 cm
Side seams
Sleeve seams
Shoulder seams

1 to 1.5 cm
Armhole/sleeve head
Waist
Panel and style lines

0.6 cm
Neckline
Collars
Facings

Imperial size chart

Based on the average figure of average height
of 5 ft 4 – 6 in

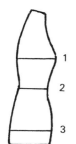

Size	10	12	14	16	18	Grade
To fit						
Bust	32	34	36	38	40	2″
Hips	34	36	38	40	42	2″

Finished measurements

		10	12	14	16	18	Grade
1	Bust	36	38	40	42	44	2″
2	Waist	$25\frac{1}{2}$	$27\frac{1}{2}$	$29\frac{1}{2}$	$31\frac{1}{2}$	$33\frac{1}{2}$	2″
3	Hips (8 in down from waist)	38	40	42	44	46	2″

Front and arm measurement

		10	12	14	16	18	Grade
1	Neck girth	$14\frac{1}{2}$	15	$15\frac{1}{2}$	16	$16\frac{1}{2}$	$\frac{1}{2}$″
2	Across chest (4 in from pit of neck)	$13\frac{1}{2}$	14	$14\frac{1}{2}$	15	$15\frac{1}{2}$	$\frac{1}{2}$″
3	Armhole circumference	16	$16\frac{1}{2}$	17	$17\frac{1}{2}$	18	$\frac{1}{2}$″
4	Upper arm girth	$12\frac{1}{2}$	13	$13\frac{1}{2}$	14	$14\frac{1}{2}$	$\frac{1}{2}$″
5	Wrist	8	$8\frac{1}{4}$	$8\frac{1}{2}$	$8\frac{3}{4}$	9	$\frac{1}{4}$″
6	Sleeve length	23	$23\frac{1}{4}$	$23\frac{1}{2}$	$23\frac{3}{4}$	24	$\frac{1}{4}$″

Back measurements, length and trouser measurements

		10	12	14	16	18	Grade
1	Shoulder length	$4\frac{3}{4}$	5	$5\frac{1}{4}$	$5\frac{1}{2}$	$5\frac{1}{2}$	
2	Across back (4 in from nape)	14	$14\frac{1}{2}$	15	$15\frac{1}{2}$	16	$\frac{1}{2}$″
3	Nape to waist	$15\frac{3}{4}$	16	$16\frac{1}{4}$	$16\frac{1}{2}$	$16\frac{3}{4}$	$\frac{1}{4}$″
4	Body rise from waist	10	$10\frac{1}{4}$	$10\frac{1}{2}$	$10\frac{3}{4}$	11	$\frac{1}{4}$″

5 Thigh level (half hip to knee) approximately $15\frac{1}{2}$ in from waist

5 Thigh girth (according to style) from $21\frac{1}{2}$ –25 in

6 Knee level 22–24 in from waist

6 Knee girth (according to style) $15\frac{1}{2}$ –$19\frac{1}{4}$ –$23\frac{1}{2}$ in

7 Outside leg (according to height) $39\frac{1}{2}$ in from waist

8 Trouser bottom width (according to style) $12\frac{1}{2}$ –$17\frac{1}{4}$ –$23\frac{1}{2}$ in

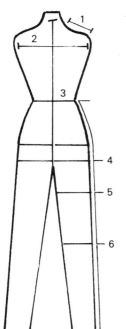

Seam allowances

$\frac{5}{8}$ to 1 in	$\frac{1}{2}$ in	$\frac{1}{4}$ in
Side seams	Armhole/sleeve head	Neckline
Sleeve seams	Waist	Collars
Shoulder seams	Panel and style lines	Facings

1 Jacket block development

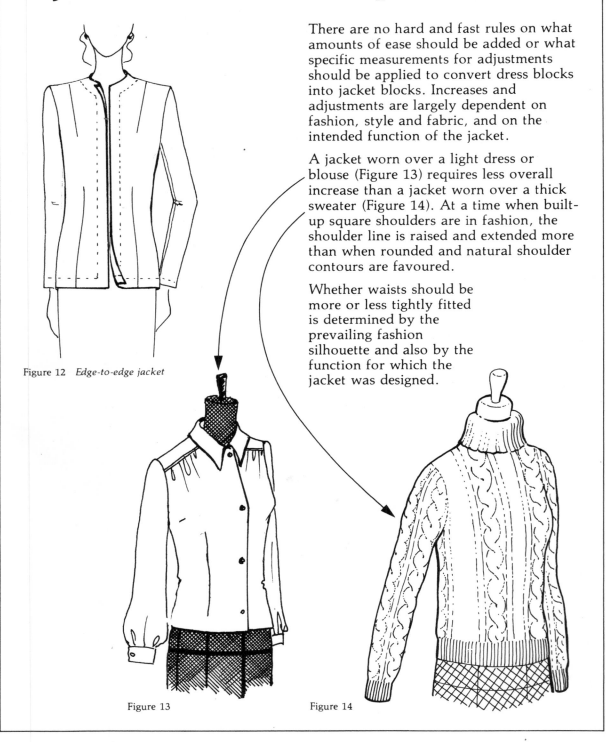

There are no hard and fast rules on what amounts of ease should be added or what specific measurements for adjustments should be applied to convert dress blocks into jacket blocks. Increases and adjustments are largely dependent on fashion, style and fabric, and on the intended function of the jacket.

A jacket worn over a light dress or blouse (Figure 13) requires less overall increase than a jacket worn over a thick sweater (Figure 14). At a time when built-up square shoulders are in fashion, the shoulder line is raised and extended more than when rounded and natural shoulder contours are favoured.

Whether waists should be more or less tightly fitted is determined by the prevailing fashion silhouette and also by the function for which the jacket was designed.

Figure 12   *Edge-to-edge jacket*

Figure 13

Figure 14

Edge-to-edge jacket

This type of jacket is developed from the *dress hip block* (use the dress hip block on page 13).

Step 1
Outline the upper part of the back and front blocks to below bust level. Shorten and reduce the depth of the front shoulder dart to 4 cm ($1\frac{1}{2}$ in) and reduce the back shoulder dart to 1 cm ($\frac{3}{8}$ in) (Figure 15(a) and (b)).

Step 2
Cut the paper, beginning on the centre front and centre back neck and shoulder lines up to the *reduced shoulder marks*. Roughly cut out the shoulder, armhole and side seam (Figure 16).

Step 3
Fold new shoulder darts, crease and pin. Draw new shoulder lines connecting the shoulder-neck points with the shoulder-armhole points. Cut on these lines, through the folded darts as shown in Figure 17.

Step 4
Unfold the darts and outline the new upper parts of the blocks. Measure back and front shoulder lines and shorten them to the original shoulder measurement (Figure 18).

'Marry' the new upper part to the remaining dress hip block.

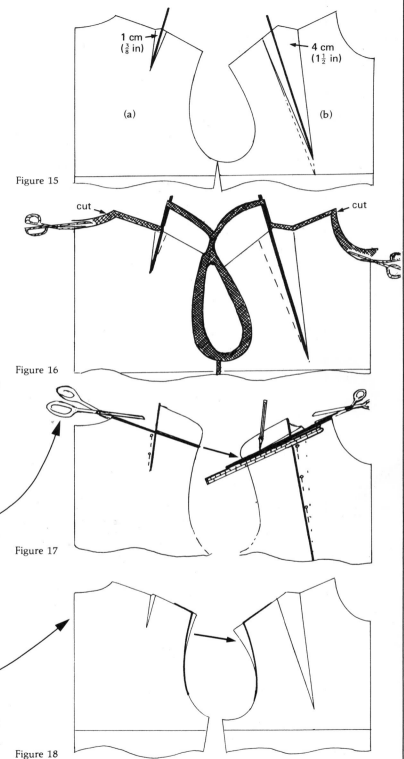

Figure 15

Figure 16

Figure 17

Figure 18

Step 5

Outline the new dress hip block with reduced depth shoulder darts. This block is now ready for further development (Figure 19).

This jacket is suitable to be worn over a thick sweater.

Step 6

Lower the necklines by 1 cm ($\frac{3}{8}$ in).

Raise the shoulder lines by 1 cm ($\frac{3}{8}$ in) at the neck points and 2 cm ($\frac{3}{4}$ in) at the armhole points and extend the shoulder lines by 1 cm ($\frac{3}{8}$ in).

Add 1 cm ($\frac{3}{8}$ in) to the side seams to increase the overall width by 4 cm ($1\frac{1}{2}$ in).

Step 7

Lower the armhole lines by 1 cm ($\frac{3}{8}$ in). This results in a larger armhole circumference, which is required for outer garments (see Table 1, on page 26). The draft is now complete (Figure 20).

Step 8

Add 3 cm ($1\frac{1}{4}$ in) seam allowances all around, except at the neckline where 1 cm ($\frac{3}{8}$ in) is sufficient. Cut out in a trial fabric similar in weight to the final fabric. Tack together for fitting.

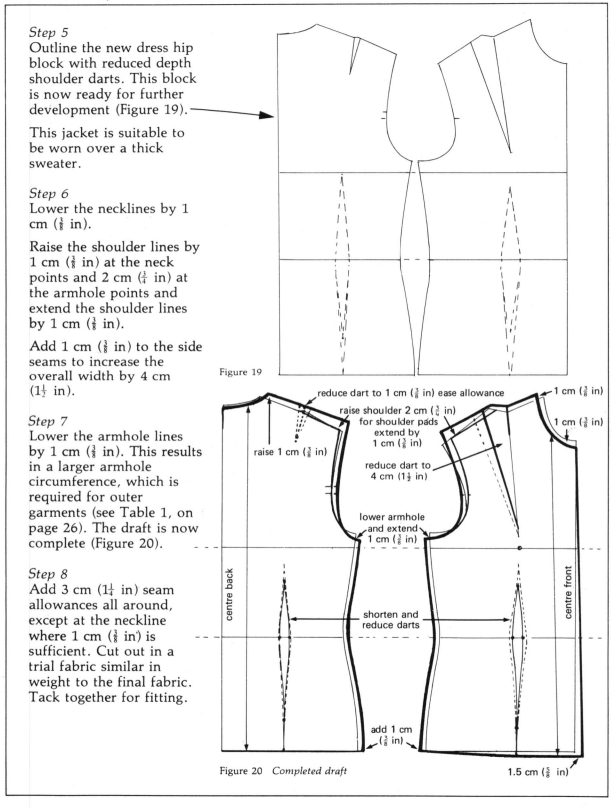

Figure 19

Figure 20 *Completed draft*

reduce dart to 1 cm ($\frac{3}{8}$ in) ease allowance

raise shoulder 2 cm ($\frac{3}{4}$ in) for shoulder pads extend by 1 cm ($\frac{3}{8}$ in)

1 cm ($\frac{3}{8}$ in)

1 cm ($\frac{3}{8}$ in)

raise 1 cm ($\frac{3}{8}$ in)

reduce dart to 4 cm ($1\frac{1}{2}$ in)

lower armhole and extend 1 cm ($\frac{3}{8}$ in)

centre back

centre front

shorten and reduce darts

add 1 cm ($\frac{3}{8}$ in)

1.5 cm ($\frac{5}{8}$ in)

Step 9
Pin a thick shoulder pad to the right shoulder of the garment-covered dress form which is the same size and thickness as the pad to be used in the making of the jacket (Figure 21).

Step 10
Fit the tacked half-jacket toile on to the dress form as shown in Figure 22. Allow the toile to hang naturally and note in particular whether the centre front and centre back edges hang in line with the centre front and centre back of the dress form.

Step 11
Raise the shoulder-neck point if the lower front and back edges hang away from the centre front and centre back of the dress form. Observe the fit of the shoulder. There must be no sagging at the armhole, so if sagging folds appear, take in the shoulder seam. Make adjustments to the neckline, side seam and darts, if required. Mark all lines and intersections carefully with a soft pencil or felt-tipped pen.

Step 12
Unpin and true all lines and seam allowances, and, if considered necessary, cut out a whole toile from the half-toile and refit. If satisfactory, transfer all marks from the toile to pattern paper or card, and develop the back neck and centre front facings (Figure 23). (See Chapter 4 of *Modelling and Flat Cutting for Fashion 1.*)

Figure 21

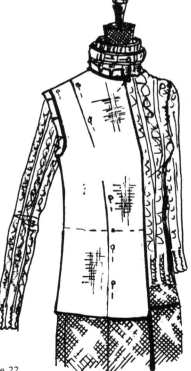

Figure 22

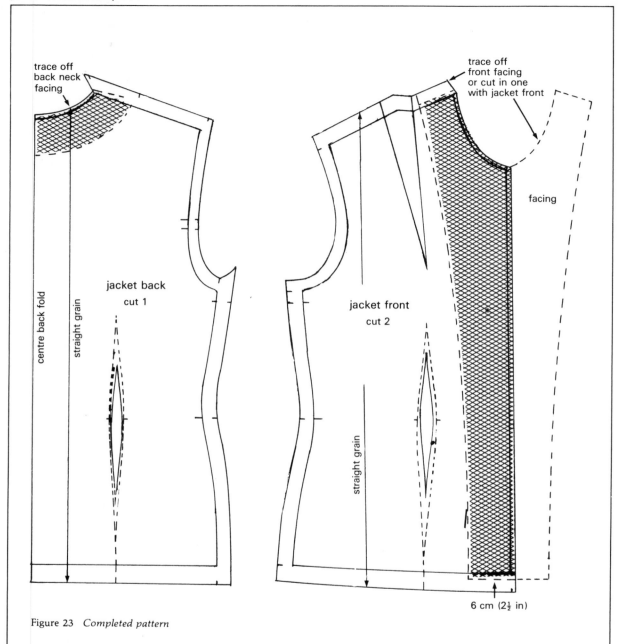

trace off
back neck
facing

trace off
front facing
or cut in one
with jacket front

facing

centre back fold

straight grain

jacket back
cut 1

jacket front
cut 2

straight grain

6 cm (2½ in)

Figure 23 *Completed pattern*

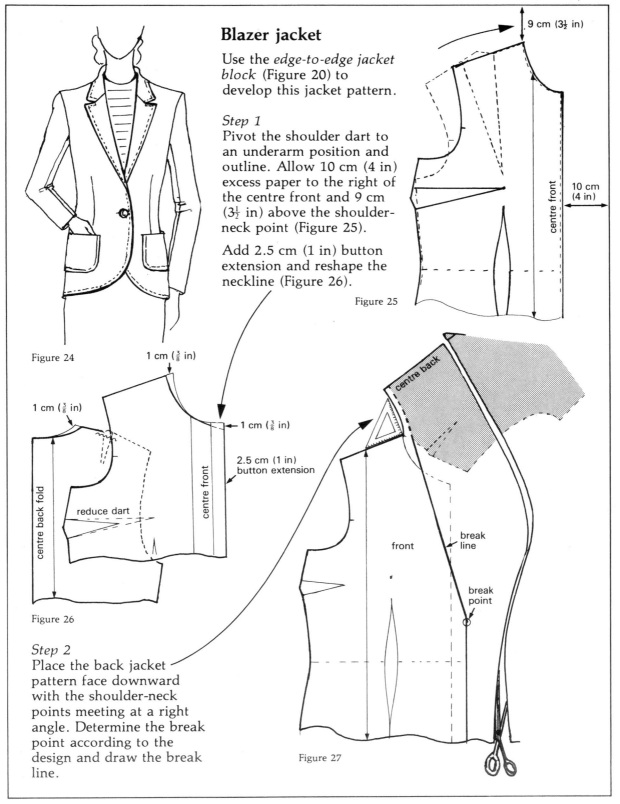

Blazer jacket

Use the *edge-to-edge jacket block* (Figure 20) to develop this jacket pattern.

Step 1
Pivot the shoulder dart to an underarm position and outline. Allow 10 cm (4 in) excess paper to the right of the centre front and 9 cm (3½ in) above the shoulder-neck point (Figure 25).

Add 2.5 cm (1 in) button extension and reshape the neckline (Figure 26).

Figure 24

Figure 25

9 cm (3½ in)

10 cm (4 in)

centre front

1 cm (⅜ in)

1 cm (⅜ in)

1 cm (⅜ in)

2.5 cm (1 in) button extension

centre back fold

centre front

reduce dart

Figure 26

centre back

front

break line

break point

Figure 27

Step 2
Place the back jacket pattern face downward with the shoulder-neck points meeting at a right angle. Determine the break point according to the design and draw the break line.

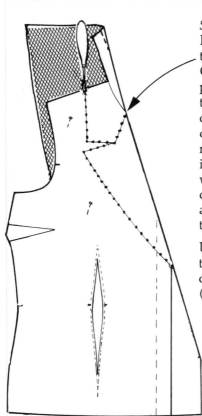

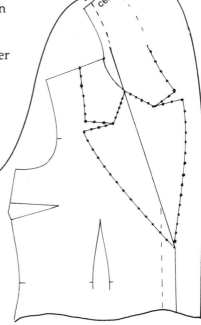

Step 3
Fold the paper under on the break line (Figure 28). Crease and pin the pattern paper (as yet incomplete) to the dress form and outline with tape a number of possible collar and revers shapes as interpreted from your working sketch. Finally, draw the desired collar and lapel shape and trace through.

Unfold the paper and tentatively complete the collar at centre back (Figure 29).

Figure 29

Figure 28

Step 4
Straighten both collar and jacket necklines as shown in Figure 30. Place balance marks and cut away the collar from the neckline and lapel line.

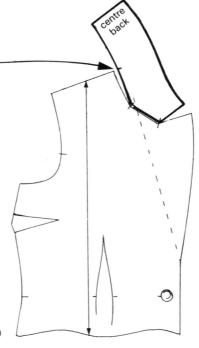

Figure 30

Step 5

Develop the top collar from the undercollar by increasing the top collar area from nothing at intersection with the lapel to 3–6 mm ($\frac{1}{8}$–$\frac{1}{4}$ in) all around the outer edge, depending on the thickness of the fabric used. See Figure 31(a) and (b).

Figure 31

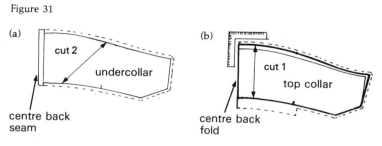

In the development of the front facing, the lapel area is increased from nothing to 3–6 mm ($\frac{1}{8}$–$\frac{1}{4}$ in) at lapel point, returning to nothing at break point. The facing area below this point is decreased by the same amount to cause the seam to roll slightly inward and be concealed.

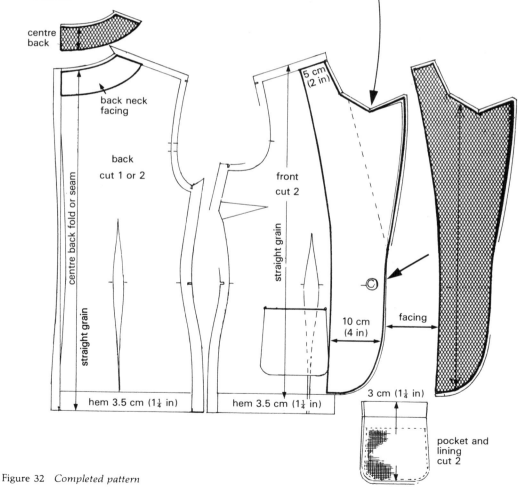

Figure 32 *Completed pattern*

Figure 33

Two-piece sleeve

This two-piece sleeve for a jacket is developed from the *dress sleeve*, and is shown in Figure 33. Table 1 gives the average measurements for a size 12 figure.

Table 1 *Size 12 average measurements*

	Dress cm	Dress in	Jacket cm	Jacket in
Armhole circumference	42	$16\frac{1}{2}$	50–52	20
Sleeve head circumference	44.5	$17\frac{1}{2}$	52–55	21
Underarm length	42	$16\frac{1}{2}$	41–43	$16\frac{1}{2}$
Upper arm girth	33	13	36–38	$14\frac{1}{2}$
Wrist girth	20.5	$8\frac{1}{4}$	28	11

Step 1

Outline the *sleeve block* (Figure 34), omitting the wrist dart. Lower the crown level line 1 cm ($\frac{3}{8}$ in) and extend to the required measurement. Raise the sleeve head and increase the wrist girth as shown. Cut out and fold the side seam edges to meet the centre line (Figure 35). Crease well and stick down. Draw the undersleeve guide lines as shown.

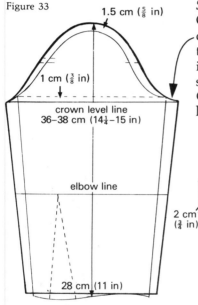

1.5 cm ($\frac{5}{8}$ in)

1 cm ($\frac{3}{8}$ in)

crown level line
36–38 cm ($14\frac{1}{4}$–15 in)

elbow line

28 cm (11 in)

Figure 34

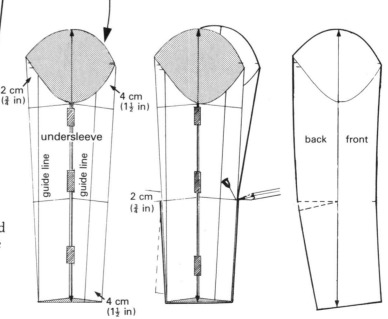

2 cm ($\frac{3}{4}$ in)

4 cm ($1\frac{1}{2}$ in)

undersleeve

guide line

guide line

2 cm ($\frac{3}{4}$ in)

4 cm ($1\frac{1}{2}$ in)

back | front

Figure 35   Figure 36   Figure 37

Step 2

On new paper, outline and trace the upper part of the folded sleeve to the elbow line and mark. Pivot the lower sleeve forward allowing 2 cm ($\frac{3}{4}$ in) additional length at the elbow level (Figure 36). Outline, and remove sleeve (Figure 37).

Step 3
Draw the shaped undersleeve (Figure 38) and trace on to pattern paper (Figure 39).

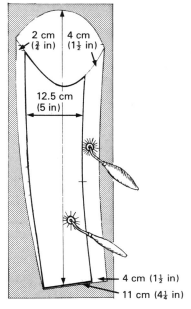

2 cm (¾ in) 4 cm (1½ in)

12.5 cm (5 in)

4 cm (1½ in)
11 cm (4¼ in)

Figure 38

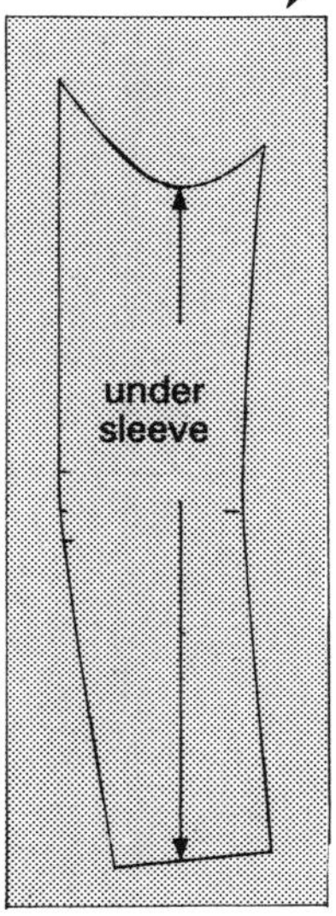

under sleeve

Figure 39

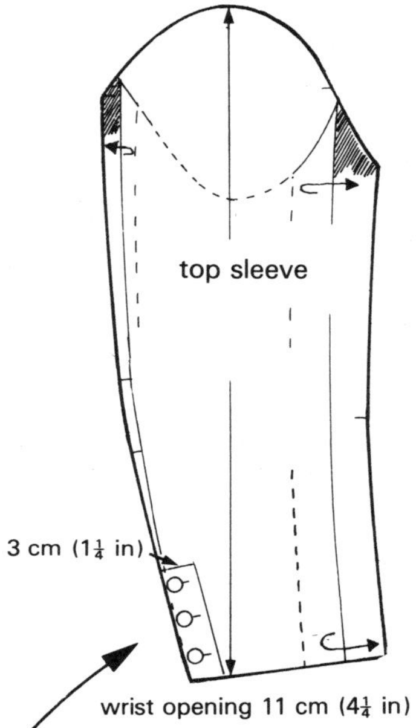

top sleeve

3 cm (1¼ in)

wrist opening 11 cm (4¼ in)

Figure 40

Step 4
Cut away the undersleeve section of the *folded sleeve* (Figure 35). Unfold the remaining sleeve and add the folded back and front sections to the sleeve (Figure 40). Outline the new top sleeve and draft optional wrist opening (Figure 40).

Step 5
Add seam and hem allowances and check balance marks and grain lines.

Step 6
Cut out in unbleached calico or other trial fabric and test the sleeve for hang and fit with the jacket. Figure 41 shows the completed pattern.

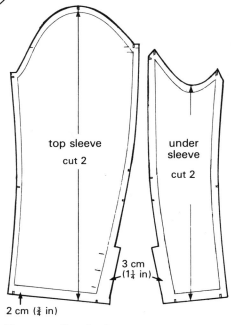

top sleeve
cut 2

under sleeve
cut 2

3 cm (1¼ in)

2 cm (¾ in)

Figure 41 *Completed pattern*

2 Trousers

Trousers are not only a useful and practical item of clothing but have now become an important garment of fashion. The one sociological factor most responsible for the great popularity of trousers in Western society is probably women's acknowledged status of equality with men regarding work and the way of life in general. Trousers have the great advantage of providing simultaneously a cover up and freedom of movement, and further lending themselves equally well to periodic fashion changes and style permutations as other articles of clothing.

As with other garments it is possible to model trousers entirely on a trouser form (Figures 42 and 43), or directly on the human figure, but a quicker and more assuredly successful method is to begin with a well-constructed basic block. Major silhouette changes (Figures 49–52) are made 'on the flat' and the pattern is then cut out in a trial fabric, for example, muslin or unbleached calico, and made up as an experimental garment, a trouser 'toile'. It is subsequently seen on a figure with the same measurements as those used in the construction of the original trouser block or on a trouser form representing these measurements.

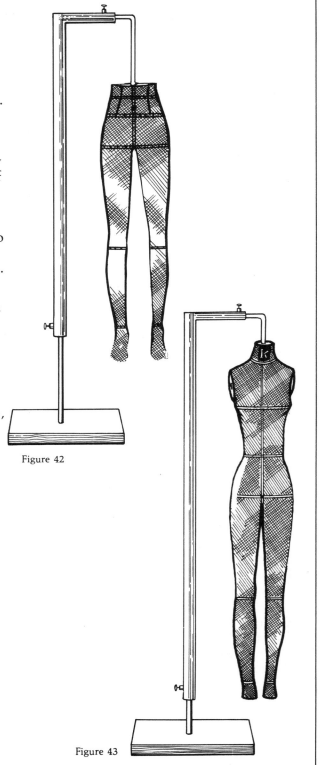

Figure 42

Figure 43

At this point three-dimensional designing begins. The fit, shape and length is checked; the placing of seams, yokes and style lines explored and marked; and the positioning of pockets, buttons and belts, use of trimmings, contrast fabric and top stitching considered in relation with the other garments that will be worn with the trousers.

The study of national characteristics and traditions, and the history and development of trousers is a most fascinating and rewarding subject for the designer, and his imagination will be stimulated by it (Figures 44–48). But most importantly, when creating new and pleasing designs, the shape of the female figure must always remain the governing factor in the designer's mind.

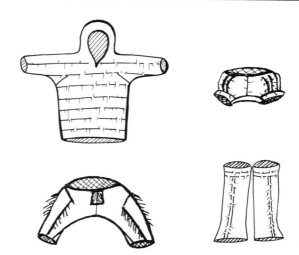

Figure 44 *Eskimos' clothing*

Figure 45 *Mandarin*

Figure 46 *Gentleman's outfit, 1818*

Figure 47 *Working woman's outfit, 1917*

Figure 48 *Country gentleman's outfit, 1927*

Figure 49   *Drain-pipe trousers*

Trouser silhouettes

The shape of trousers is influenced mainly by the prevailing fashion silhouette, particularly that of the skirt, but also by the function for which they are intended, and the fabric to be used.

Ankle-hugging 'drain-pipes' (Figure 49) develop into 'flared bottoms' (Figure 50), often with the introduction of seams.

'Pencil' trousers are straight throughout, yet slim-fitting at the waist and hips (Figure 51).

'Oxford bags' hang straight and loose, with characteristic pleats at the waist line (Figure 52).

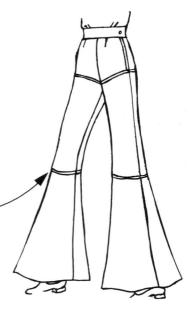

Figure 50   *Flared trousers*

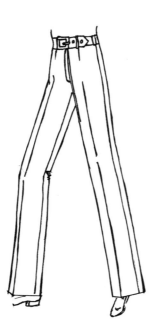

Figure 51   *Pencil trousers*

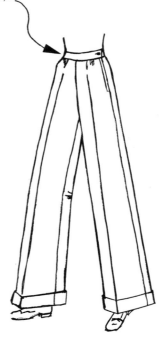

Figure 52   *Oxford bags*

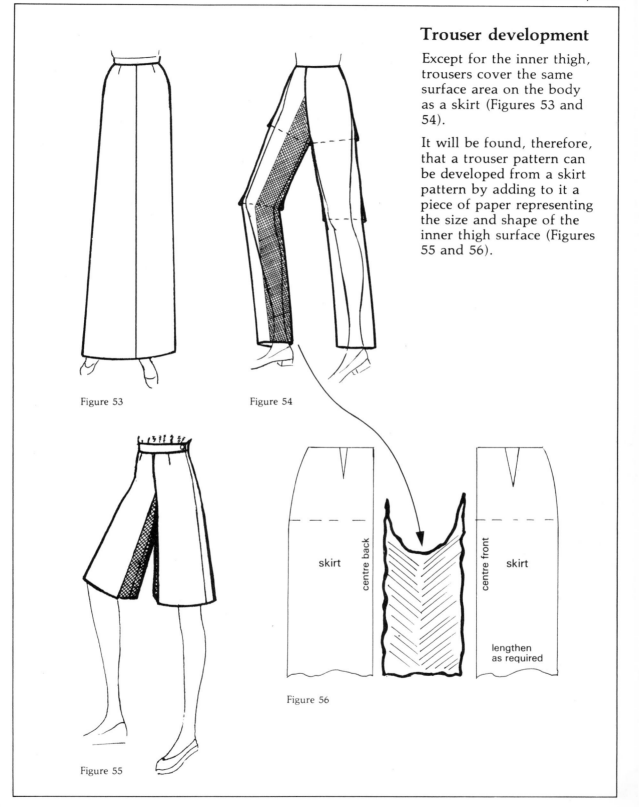

Trouser development

Except for the inner thigh, trousers cover the same surface area on the body as a skirt (Figures 53 and 54).

It will be found, therefore, that a trouser pattern can be developed from a skirt pattern by adding to it a piece of paper representing the size and shape of the inner thigh surface (Figures 55 and 56).

Figure 53

Figure 54

Figure 55

Figure 56

skirt

centre back

centre front

skirt

lengthen
as required

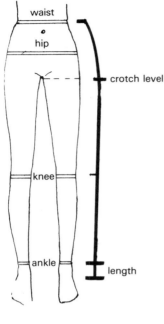

Figure 57

Constructing the trouser block

This trouser block is developed from the *straight skirt block* shown in Figure 58. See also the scale blocks on page 14.

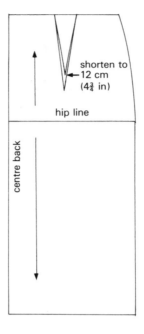

from   waist

shorten to
12 cm
(4¾ in)

hip line

centre back

to

knee level
58 cm (22¾ in)

Figure 58

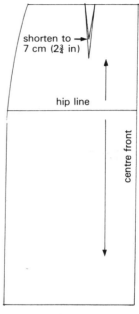

shorten to →
7 cm (2¾ in)

hip line

centre front

To fit waist 66 cm (26 in)
hip 94 cm (37 in)

As the skirt blocks already contain the basic shape and measurements, only three more measurements are required to construct the *basic trouser block*. These are:

1 Outside leg
2 Body rise or crotch level
3 Width of trouser bottom

For comparison of other measurements see the size charts on pages 16 and 17.

Figure 59 *Basic trousers*

The position of the *crotch level* is determined primarily by the body rise measurement (Figure 60). Added to this measurement is a variable amount of tolerance for ease of movement and comfort in wear. See Table 2.

The actual amount allowed over and above the body measurements is influenced by a number of factors: the function for which the trousers are intended and the fabric that is to be used, for example, soft stretch fabric instead of a bulky fabric. Probably the most decisive factor regarding everyday-wear garments is the prevailing fashion mood which will 'date' more than anything a trouser crotch line that is considered too high or too low.

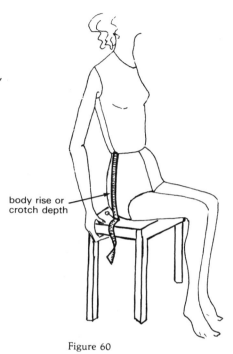

body rise or crotch depth

Figure 60

Table 2 *Average ease allowances on body rise measurements*

Size	10		12		14		16		18	
	cm	in	cm	in	cm	in	cm	in	cm	in
Body rise	25.5	10	26	$10\frac{1}{4}$	26.5	$10\frac{1}{2}$	27	$10\frac{3}{4}$	28	11
With ease	28	11	28.5	$11\frac{1}{4}$	29	$11\frac{1}{2}$	29.5	$11\frac{3}{4}$	30.5	12

Measurements for constructing the size 12 trouser blocks are:

Waist	66 cm (26 in)	⎫
Hip	94 cm (37 in)	⎬ skirt measurements
Knee length	58 cm (22¾ in)	⎭
Outside leg	102 cm (40 in)	
Crotch level from waist	28 cm (11 in)	
Bottom of trousers width	60 cm (23½ in)	

Step 1
Draw a vertical line 102 cm (40 in) long and 15 cm (6 in) away from the edge of the paper and parallel to it (Figure 61).

Step 2
Place the *back skirt block* on the paper with the centre back touching the vertical line. Outline to knee level.

Step 3
Extend waist, hip and knee level lines across the paper.

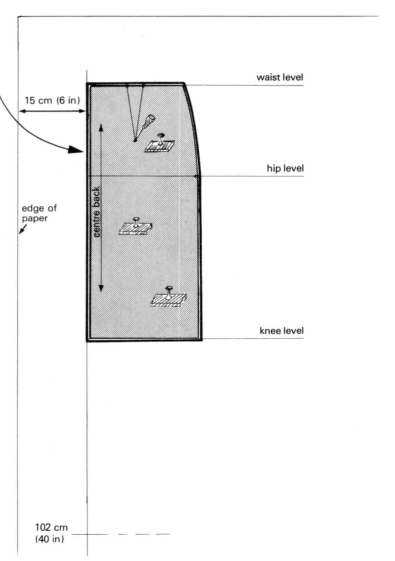

15 cm (6 in)

edge of paper

centre back

waist level

hip level

knee level

102 cm (40 in)

Figure 61

Step 4
Place the *front skirt block* to the back side seam line with all level lines aligning, and outline. Lengthen and complete centre front, side seam and bottom of trousers lines.

Step 5
Draw the crotch line 28 cm (11 in) down from the waist line and parallel to it. Extend this line 12 cm (4¾ in) beyond centre back* and 7 cm (2¾ in) beyond centre front** and square down to bottom of trousers.

The amounts allowed for extensions are based on the average inside thigh measurement and are further influenced by the depth of the crotch level (the higher the level the longer the extension).

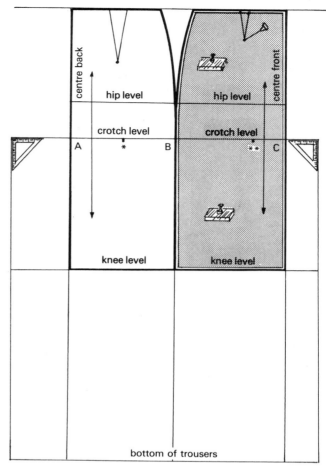

Figure 62

* Back extension equals half the back crotch line, for example, A–B = 24 cm (9½ in). Half A–B = 12 cm (4¾ in). See Table 3.

** Front extension equals one quarter of the front crotch line plus 1 cm (⅜ in), for example, B–C = 25 cm (10 in). Quarter B–C = 6.3 cm + 1 cm = 7.3 cm (2⅞ in) to nearest unit. See Table 3.

Table 3 *Example of crotch line extensions*

Size	10		12		14	
	cm	*in*	*cm*	*in*	*cm*	*in*
Back	11.5	4½	12	4¾	12.5	5
Front	7	2¾	7.3	2⅞	7.5	3

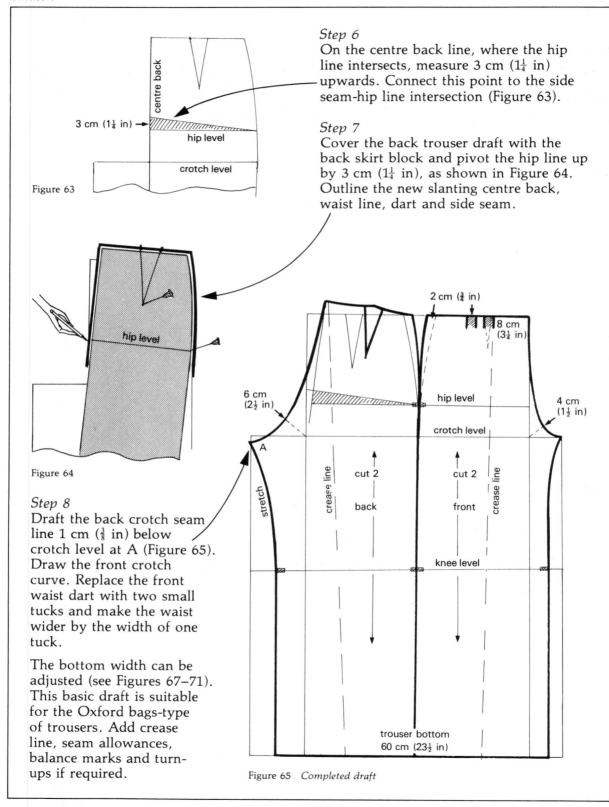

Step 6
On the centre back line, where the hip line intersects, measure 3 cm (1¼ in) upwards. Connect this point to the side seam-hip line intersection (Figure 63).

Step 7
Cover the back trouser draft with the back skirt block and pivot the hip line up by 3 cm (1¼ in), as shown in Figure 64. Outline the new slanting centre back, waist line, dart and side seam.

Figure 63

centre back

3 cm (1¼ in)

hip level

crotch level

Figure 64

hip level

Step 8
Draft the back crotch seam line 1 cm (⅜ in) below crotch level at A (Figure 65). Draw the front crotch curve. Replace the front waist dart with two small tucks and make the waist wider by the width of one tuck.

The bottom width can be adjusted (see Figures 67–71). This basic draft is suitable for the Oxford bags-type of trousers. Add crease line, seam allowances, balance marks and turn-ups if required.

2 cm (¾ in)

8 cm (3¼ in)

6 cm (2½ in)

hip level

4 cm (1½ in)

crotch level

A

stretch

crease line

cut 2

back

cut 2

front

crease line

knee level

trouser bottom
60 cm (23½ in)

Figure 65 *Completed draft*

Trouser block adaptations

Standard width trousers
Outline the *basic trouser block* (Figure 65). Reduce the knee and bottom width as shown in Figure 67, and hollow out slightly the front and back crotch seam to obtain a closer fit.

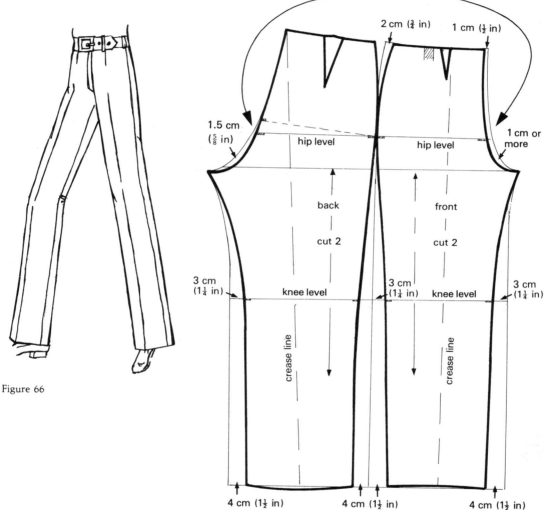

Figure 66

Figure 67 *Completed draft*

Table 4 *Standard width trouser measurements*

Size	10		12		14	
	cm	in	cm	in	cm	in
Knee width	48	$18\frac{3}{4}$	49	$19\frac{1}{4}$	50	$19\frac{3}{4}$
Bottom width	43	$16\frac{3}{4}$	44	$17\frac{1}{4}$	45	$17\frac{3}{4}$

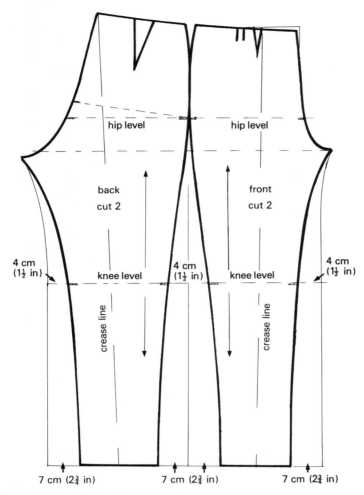

hip level   hip level

back
cut 2

front
cut 2

4 cm
(1½ in)

4 cm
(1½ in)

4 cm
(1½ in)

knee level   knee level

crease line   crease line

7 cm (2¾ in)   7 cm (2¾ in)   7 cm (2¾ in)

Figure 68   *Completed pattern*

Tapered trousers
Outline the *basic trouser block* (Figure 65). Reduce knee and bottom width as shown in Figure 68. The bottom width is 2–3 cm (1 in) wider than the ankle measurement.

Figure 69

Table 5   *Tapered width trouser measurements*

Size	10		12		14	
	cm	in	cm	in	cm	in
Knee width	43	16¾	44	17¼	45	17¾
Bottom width	31	12	32	12½	33	13

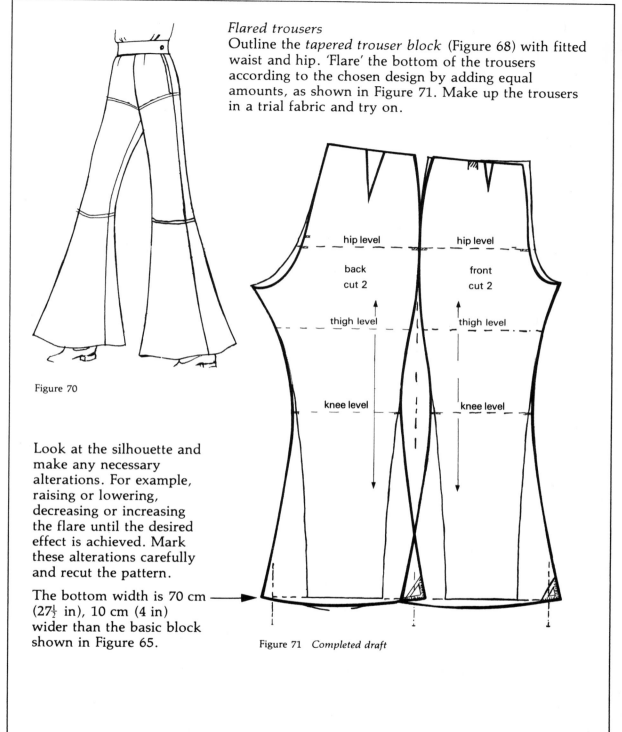

Flared trousers
Outline the *tapered trouser block* (Figure 68) with fitted waist and hip. 'Flare' the bottom of the trousers according to the chosen design by adding equal amounts, as shown in Figure 71. Make up the trousers in a trial fabric and try on.

Figure 70

Look at the silhouette and make any necessary alterations. For example, raising or lowering, decreasing or increasing the flare until the desired effect is achieved. Mark these alterations carefully and recut the pattern.

The bottom width is 70 cm (27½ in), 10 cm (4 in) wider than the basic block shown in Figure 65.

Figure 71 *Completed draft*

Fitting the trouser block

The basic trouser blocks shown in Figures
65–71 are drafted to the average stock
size measurements, and the resulting
patterns fit the majority of women with
such measurements. Due to differences of
body structure in women who otherwise
have identical waist and hip
measurements, variations in fit may
occur, and, therefore, alterations are
required. Other reasons for a designer
wishing to adapt the fit of trouser blocks
are the changes of styles and fashion
silhouettes.

*Examples of the most frequently
encountered alterations*
Very tight-fitting trousers have fitting
problems entirely divorced from the
usual adjustments. Unless a stretch
material is used, or a seam or horizontal
dart introduced, it is impossible to fit
trousers immediately below the seat
without wrinkles appearing in that area
(Figure 72). This fitting problem is again
encountered when trousers are expected
to flare out suddenly from a previously
leg-hugging fit without causing the side
seam to pull, so a seam placed in this
position is a great fitting aid. Oxford
bags are much easier to fit provided
sufficient fulness for pleats at waist level
is allowed (Figures 73 and 74).

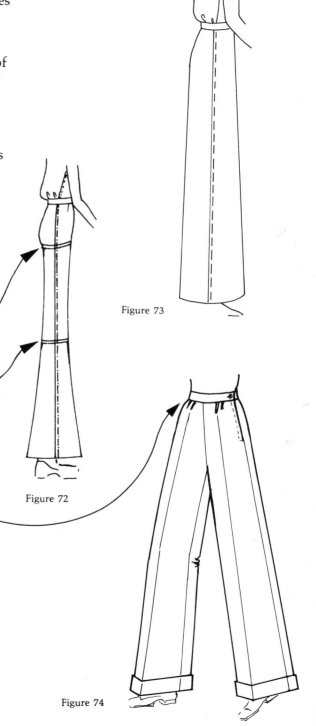

Figure 73

Figure 72

Figure 74

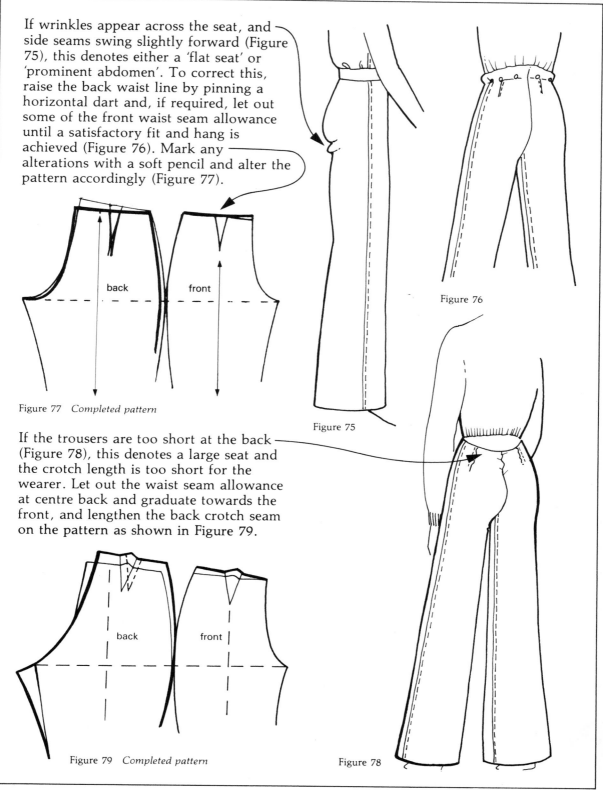

If wrinkles appear across the seat, and side seams swing slightly forward (Figure 75), this denotes either a 'flat seat' or 'prominent abdomen'. To correct this, raise the back waist line by pinning a horizontal dart and, if required, let out some of the front waist seam allowance until a satisfactory fit and hang is achieved (Figure 76). Mark any alterations with a soft pencil and alter the pattern accordingly (Figure 77).

back   front

Figure 77 *Completed pattern*

Figure 76

Figure 75

If the trousers are too short at the back (Figure 78), this denotes a large seat and the crotch length is too short for the wearer. Let out the waist seam allowance at centre back and graduate towards the front, and lengthen the back crotch seam on the pattern as shown in Figure 79.

back   front

Figure 79 *Completed pattern*

Figure 78

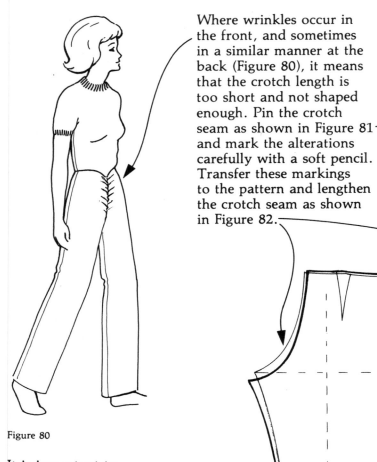

Where wrinkles occur in the front, and sometimes in a similar manner at the back (Figure 80), it means that the crotch length is too short and not shaped enough. Pin the crotch seam as shown in Figure 81 and mark the alterations carefully with a soft pencil. Transfer these markings to the pattern and lengthen the crotch seam as shown in Figure 82.

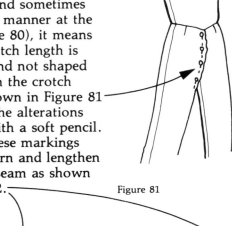

Figure 81

Figure 80

It is important to remember to always assemble one trouser leg at a time and to stitch the crotch seam last of all (Figure 83).

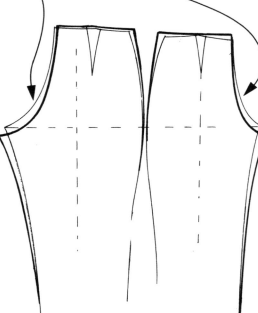

Figure 82 *Completed alteration*

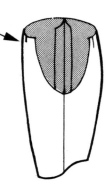

Figure 83

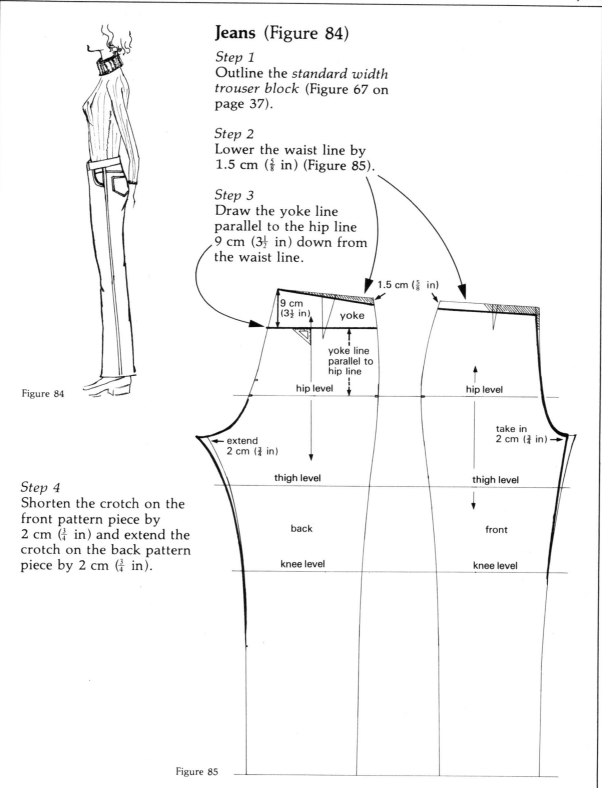

Jeans (Figure 84)

Step 1
Outline the *standard width trouser block* (Figure 67 on page 37).

Step 2
Lower the waist line by 1.5 cm ($\frac{5}{8}$ in) (Figure 85).

Step 3
Draw the yoke line parallel to the hip line 9 cm ($3\frac{1}{2}$ in) down from the waist line.

Step 4
Shorten the crotch on the front pattern piece by 2 cm ($\frac{3}{4}$ in) and extend the crotch on the back pattern piece by 2 cm ($\frac{3}{4}$ in).

Figure 84

1.5 cm ($\frac{5}{8}$ in)

9 cm ($3\frac{1}{2}$ in)

yoke

yoke line parallel to hip line

hip level

hip level

extend 2 cm ($\frac{3}{4}$ in)

take in 2 cm ($\frac{3}{4}$ in)

thigh level

thigh level

back

front

knee level

knee level

Figure 85

Step 5
Complete the draft by drawing in all the relevant information: position and size of back and front pockets; trouser fly and zip guard (Figures 86 and 87).

Step 6
Trace all the pattern sections on to a new sheet of paper, including grain lines and balance marks (Figure 88).

Add seam allowances.

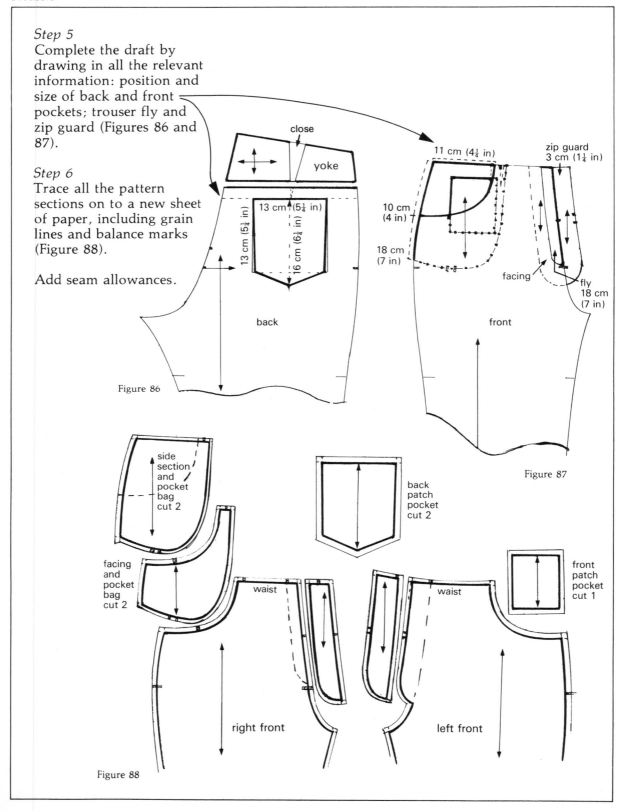

close

yoke

13 cm (5¼ in)

13 cm (5¼ in)

16 cm (6¼ in)

back

Figure 86

11 cm (4¼ in)

zip guard
3 cm (1¼ in)

10 cm (4 in)

18 cm (7 in)

facing

front

fly
18 cm (7 in)

Figure 87

side section and pocket bag cut 2

facing and pocket bag cut 2

waist

back patch pocket cut 2

waist

front patch pocket cut 1

right front

left front

Figure 88

Step 7
The trouser belt is 4 cm (1½ in) wide. Cut on the fold or with a seam added if a finer fabric facing is used (Figure 89).

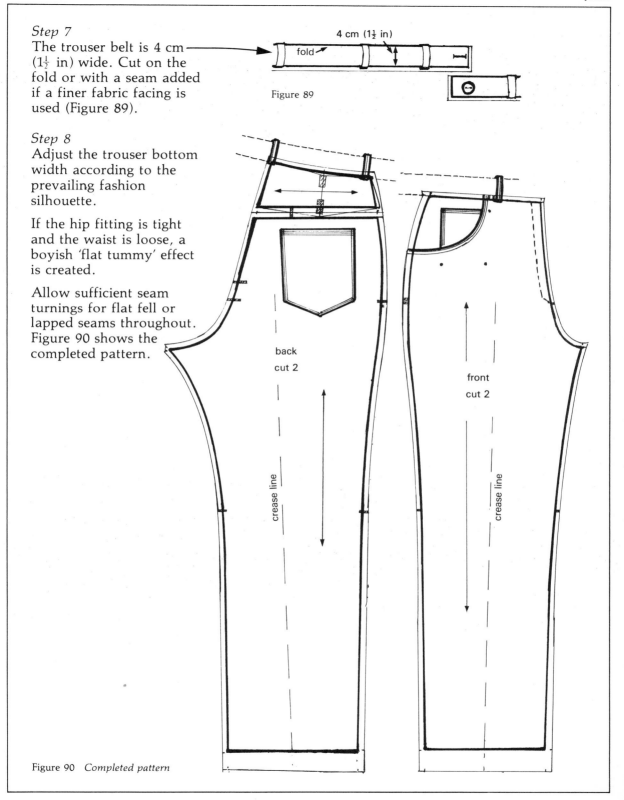

Figure 89

Step 8
Adjust the trouser bottom width according to the prevailing fashion silhouette.

If the hip fitting is tight and the waist is loose, a boyish 'flat tummy' effect is created.

Allow sufficient seam turnings for flat fell or lapped seams throughout. Figure 90 shows the completed pattern.

4 cm (1½ in)

fold

back
cut 2

front
cut 2

crease line

crease line

Figure 90   *Completed pattern*

Bloomers

An American lady, Amelia Jenks Bloomer, was responsible for the creation of the bloomer suit, and for the success it enjoyed with female cyclists in the second half of the nineteenth century.

The fashionable twill bathing-suit of 1890 (Figure 91) was adapted from the long, tailored jacket and knee-length baggy pants of the bloomer suit.

The cami-bockers (Figure 92) appeared in 1929.

The gradual merging of the style of bloomers with those of the then new divided skirt, and later the trousers, led to a more fitted garment which retained the characteristic fulness at the bottom of the trouser leg (Figures 93 and 94).

By using a basic block, new designs can be created, based on the demands of fashion trends and functional needs.

Figure 91   *Twill bathing-costume, 1890*

Figure 92   *Cami-bockers, 1929*

Figure 93   *'Siren suit', 1940*

Figure 94   *Fashionable 'bloomers', 1975*

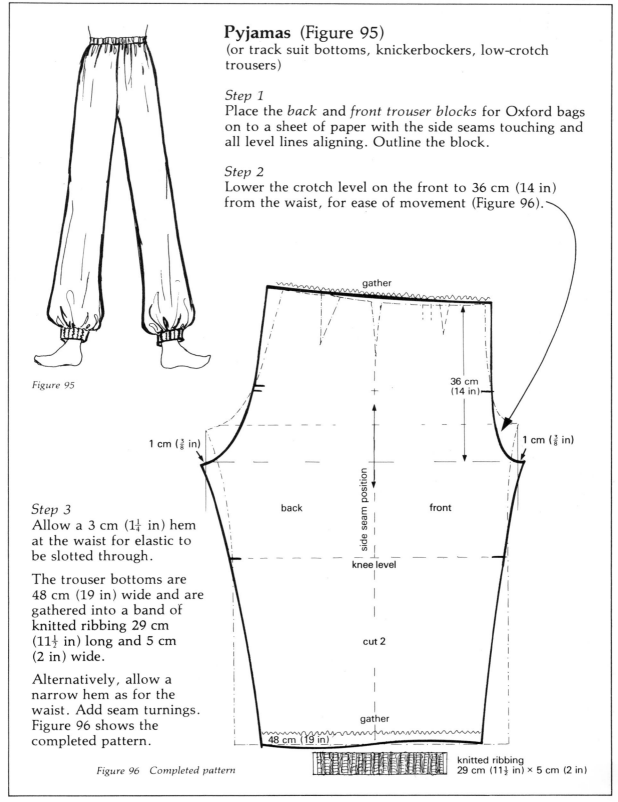

Pyjamas (Figure 95)

(or track suit bottoms, knickerbockers, low-crotch trousers)

Step 1
Place the *back* and *front trouser blocks* for Oxford bags on to a sheet of paper with the side seams touching and all level lines aligning. Outline the block.

Step 2
Lower the crotch level on the front to 36 cm (14 in) from the waist, for ease of movement (Figure 96).

Figure 95

gather

1 cm ($\frac{3}{8}$ in)

36 cm (14 in)

1 cm ($\frac{3}{8}$ in)

back

side seam position

front

knee level

cut 2

gather

48 cm (19 in)

knitted ribbing
29 cm (11½ in) × 5 cm (2 in)

Step 3
Allow a 3 cm (1¼ in) hem at the waist for elastic to be slotted through.

The trouser bottoms are 48 cm (19 in) wide and are gathered into a band of knitted ribbing 29 cm (11½ in) long and 5 cm (2 in) wide.

Alternatively, allow a narrow hem as for the waist. Add seam turnings. Figure 96 shows the completed pattern.

Figure 96   Completed pattern

47

Jodhpur trousers

Step 1
Draw on pattern paper a horizontal line representing the trouser crotch level. Place the *back* and *front tapered leg trouser blocks* (Figure 68) on to the paper aligning the crotch level lines. Outline as shown.

Step 2
Lower the crotch level lines and crotch points by 4 cm (1½ in) and extend widths by the amounts given.

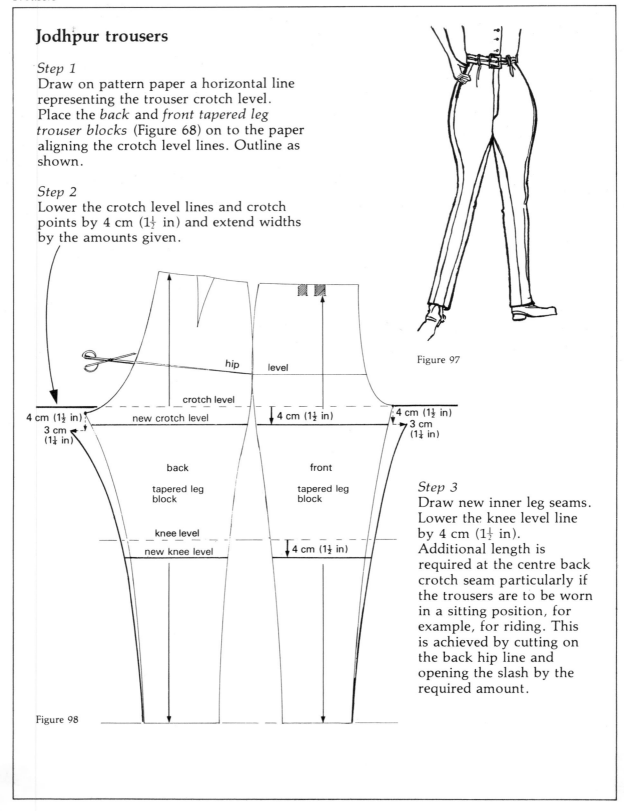

Figure 97

Figure 98

hip level

crotch level

new crotch level

4 cm (1½ in)

4 cm (1½ in)
3 cm (1¼ in)

4 cm (1½ in)
3 cm (1¼ in)

back
tapered leg block

front
tapered leg block

knee level

new knee level

4 cm (1½ in)

4 cm (1½ in)

Step 3
Draw new inner leg seams. Lower the knee level line by 4 cm (1½ in). Additional length is required at the centre back crotch seam particularly if the trousers are to be worn in a sitting position, for example, for riding. This is achieved by cutting on the back hip line and opening the slash by the required amount.

Step 4
Cut on the back hip level line from centre back to side seam. Open the slash 3 cm ($1\frac{1}{4}$ in) and outline the new centre back crotch seam line and back waist line, including the waist dart (Figure 99).

The trouser block is now ready for development into jodhpur-style trousers.

Jodhpur trousers and breeches are sometimes in fashion, but primarily they are being worn for riding and other sports activities. The wearer must feel comfortable in movement and in a sitting position.

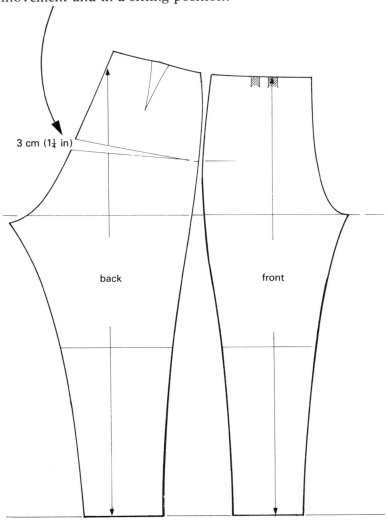

3 cm ($1\frac{1}{4}$ in)

back

front

Figure 99

Step 5
Shape the side seams as shown in Figure 100. Add seam allowances, balance marks, grain lines and cutting instructions.

Step 6
Cut out in calico allowing large seam turnings for possible adjustment. Fit on a figure to see the trousers in movement.

Fulness around the hip area can be reduced or increased as desired until a satisfactory effect is achieved. Add pockets, waistband and, if required, a fly-front opening.

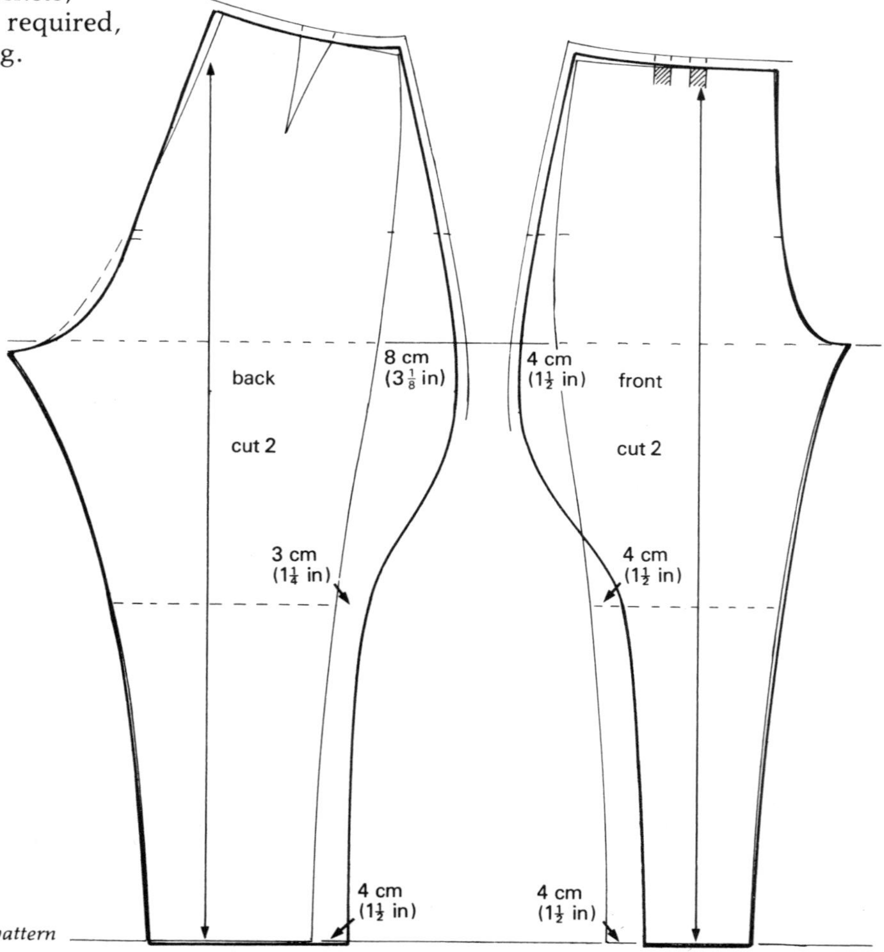

back

cut 2

8 cm
(3 $\frac{1}{8}$ in)

4 cm
(1 $\frac{1}{2}$ in)   front

cut 2

3 cm
(1 $\frac{1}{4}$ in)

4 cm
(1 $\frac{1}{2}$ in)

4 cm
(1 $\frac{1}{2}$ in)

4 cm
(1 $\frac{1}{2}$ in)

Figure 100 *Completed pattern*

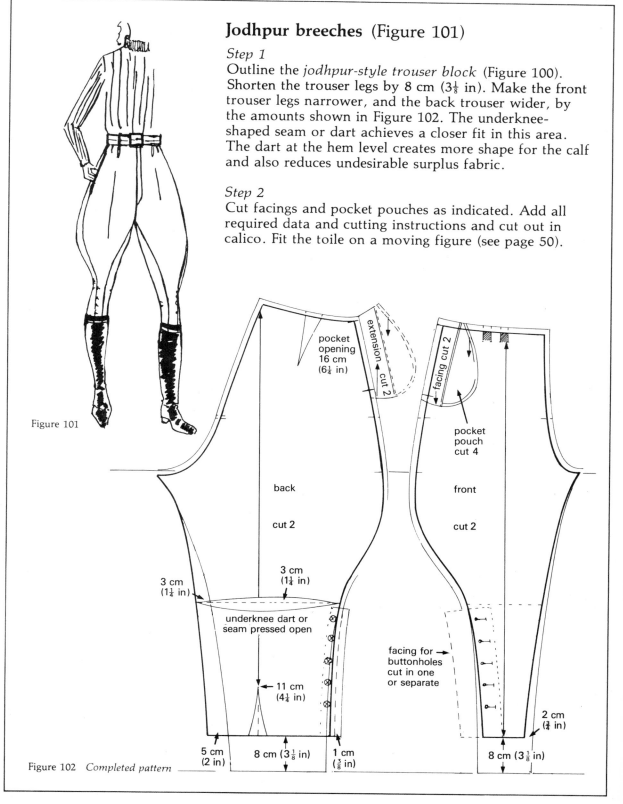

Jodhpur breeches (Figure 101)

Step 1
Outline the *jodhpur-style trouser block* (Figure 100). Shorten the trouser legs by 8 cm (3⅛ in). Make the front trouser legs narrower, and the back trouser wider, by the amounts shown in Figure 102. The underknee-shaped seam or dart achieves a closer fit in this area. The dart at the hem level creates more shape for the calf and also reduces undesirable surplus fabric.

Step 2
Cut facings and pocket pouches as indicated. Add all required data and cutting instructions and cut out in calico. Fit the toile on a moving figure (see page 50).

Figure 101

pocket opening 16 cm (6¼ in)

extension cut 2

facing cut 2

pocket pouch cut 4

back
cut 2

front
cut 2

3 cm (1¼ in)

3 cm (1¼ in)

underknee dart or seam pressed open

facing for → buttonholes cut in one or separate

11 cm (4¼ in)

2 cm (¾ in)

5 cm (2 in)

8 cm (3⅛ in)

1 cm (⅜ in)

8 cm (3⅛ in)

Figure 102 *Completed pattern*

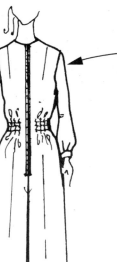

Figure 103

Jumpsuit (Figure 103)

Step 1
Use the *hip block* (page 13) and the *trouser block* (Figure 65 on page 36) and draft on to a sheet of paper measuring 150 cm by 90 cm (59 in by $35\frac{1}{2}$ in) for a full-length jumpsuit.

Step 2
Draw the centre back line 15 cm (6 in) away from the left-hand side of the paper and parallel to it. Square out a line as shown in Figure 104.

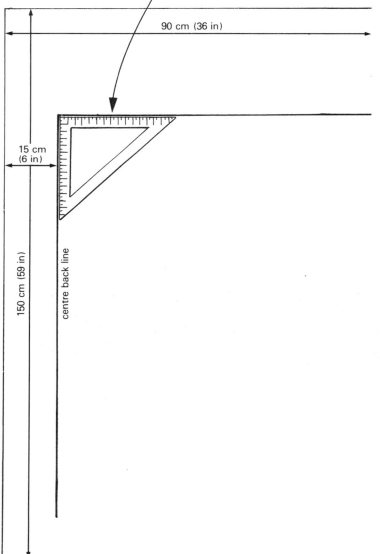

Figure 104

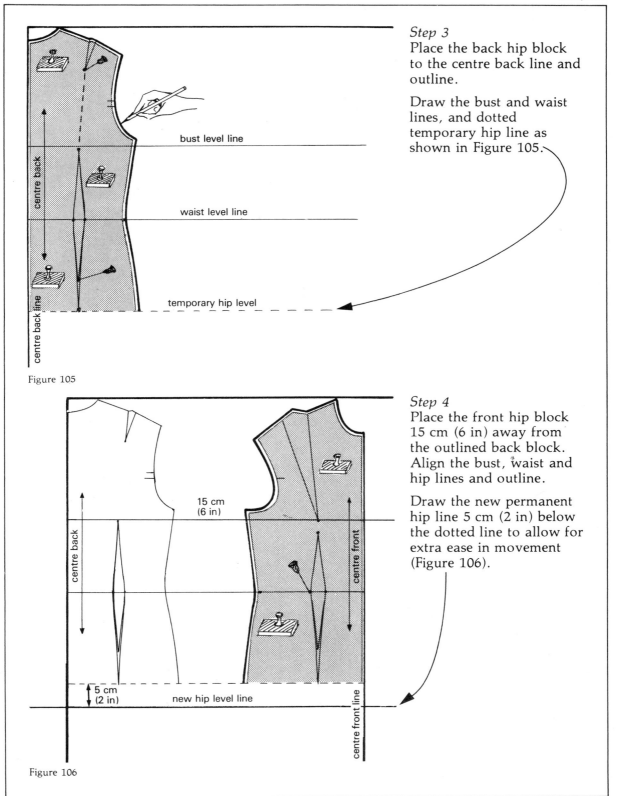

Figure 105

Figure 106

Step 3
Place the back hip block to the centre back line and outline.

Draw the bust and waist lines, and dotted temporary hip line as shown in Figure 105.

Step 4
Place the front hip block 15 cm (6 in) away from the outlined back block. Align the bust, waist and hip lines and outline.

Draw the new permanent hip line 5 cm (2 in) below the dotted line to allow for extra ease in movement (Figure 106).

Step 5
Lengthen the centre back and centre front lines to the full-length of the jumpsuit. Join the hip and trouser blocks by aligning the trouser hip lines with those of the hip blocks; and align the centre front and centre back lines with the centre back and centre front lines of the back and front hip blocks (Figure 107).

Outline and remove the trouser blocks.

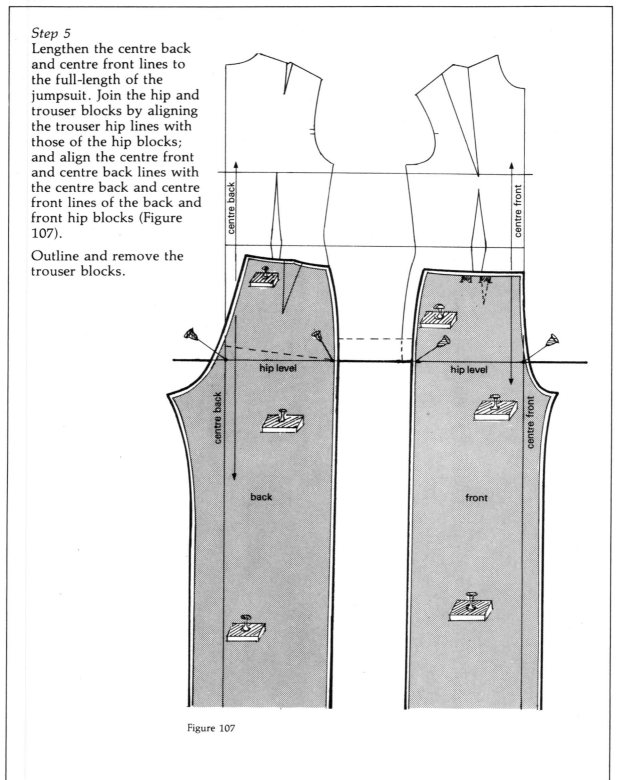

Figure 107

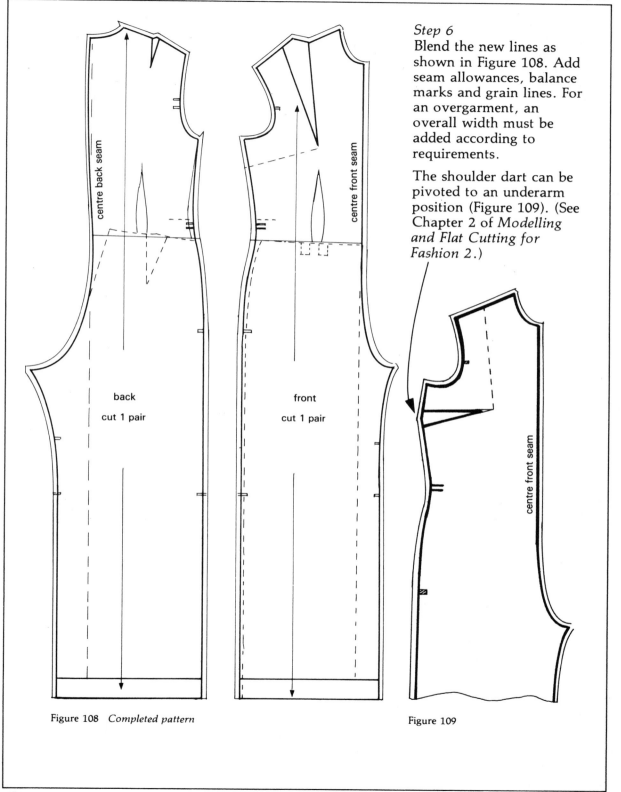

Step 6
Blend the new lines as shown in Figure 108. Add seam allowances, balance marks and grain lines. For an overgarment, an overall width must be added according to requirements.

The shoulder dart can be pivoted to an underarm position (Figure 109). (See Chapter 2 of *Modelling and Flat Cutting for Fashion 2*.)

centre back seam

centre front seam

back

cut 1 pair

front

cut 1 pair

centre front seam

Figure 108   *Completed pattern*

Figure 109

Dungarees

Made in strong denim, khaki and
drilling, overalls and dungarees were (and
still are) worn as protective overgarments
by men at work. During the Second
World War, factory girls tackled the jobs
of men, and began to wear slacks and
dungarees (Figure 110). Today, dungarees
have become a fashion garment for
women, with a unisex look, and their
function is now perhaps associated more
with leisure rather than work. By their
nature, dungarees still remain loose and
unrestricting, but the fabrics in which
they are now being made are often lighter
in weight and more varied in colour and
design.

The dungarees shown in Figure 113 are
cut flat, but pattern parts can be tried out
on the figure or on the dress form, in
paper or in modelling material, until the
desired effect is achieved (Figures 111 and
112).

Figure 110 *Dungarees, 1939*

can be tried out
on the figure

or on the
dress form

Figure 111

Figure 112

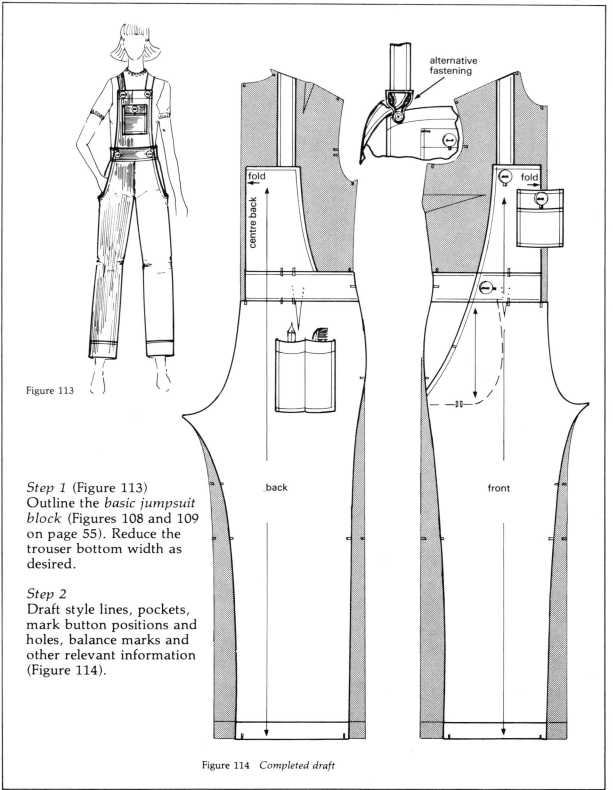

Figure 113

Step 1 (Figure 113)
Outline the *basic jumpsuit block* (Figures 108 and 109 on page 55). Reduce the trouser bottom width as desired.

Step 2
Draft style lines, pockets, mark button positions and holes, balance marks and other relevant information (Figure 114).

alternative fastening

fold

centre back

back

fold

front

Figure 114   *Completed draft*

Step 3
Trace the pattern sections on to new
paper and add seam allowances only
where required, according to seam type
(Figure 115).

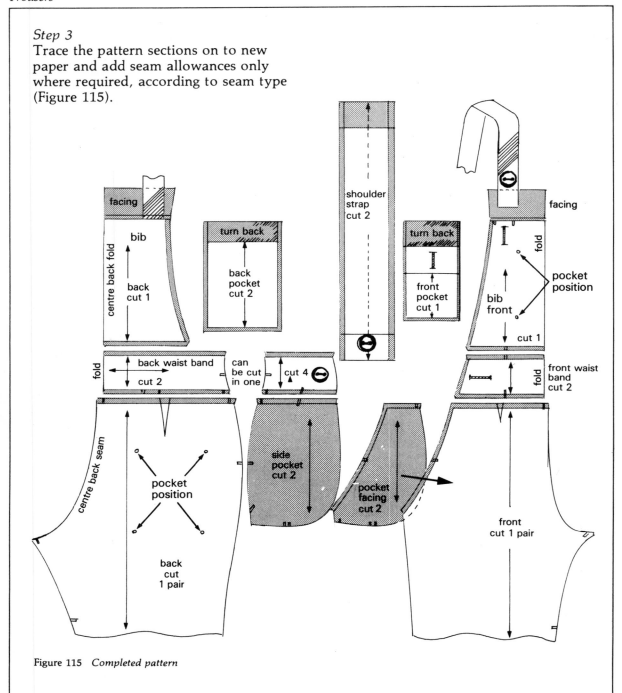

Figure 115 *Completed pattern*

Figure 116

Ski-suit (or jumpsuit)

The function of this suit must be carefully considered before the pattern is made. A ski-suit is an outer garment worn over layers of other clothing, and is worn for all types of winter sports. Therefore, it must be loosely-fitting and allow for much ease in movement. The one-piece nature of the garment has the advantage of keeping out rain, snow and cold winds, but also has the disadvantage of restricting movement at waist level when a person bends forward or sits down, so allowances must be made for this.

This ski- or jumpsuit is based on the basic jumpsuit construction (Figures 108 and 109) which has extra length allowed from the nape to waist, and from the waist to crotch level. For the ski-suit it is recommended that the low-level crotch line of the track suit trousers (Figure 96) is used. Additional width, according to requirements, must be added to the basic jumpsuit before development. The ski-suit shown in Figure 116 has elasticated straps at the wrists and ankles, and has an elasticated waist belt. A long zip at the back waist line can be included in the design (Figure 117).

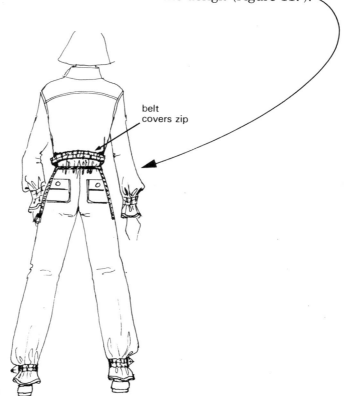

belt covers zip

Figure 117

Step 1

Outline the *basic jumpsuit* (Figures 108 and 109 on page 55). Add an extra width throughout as required. Reduce the width of the trouser bottoms to 50 cm ($19\frac{3}{4}$ in) or 55 cm ($21\frac{1}{2}$ in). Lower the neckline all round by 2 cm ($\frac{3}{4}$ in). Tentatively draw the yoke lines, positions of the waist line and pockets. Cut out the pattern pieces and pin the back and front shoulder and side seams together using a right side 'lapped seam' effect. Pin this shell to the dress form (Figure 118).

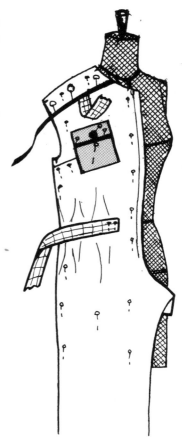

Figure 118

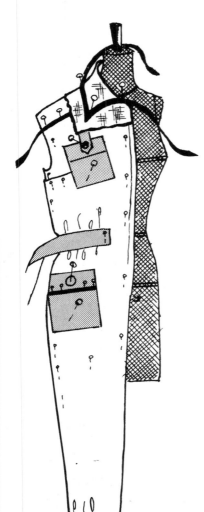

Figure 119

Step 2

With tape, outline the most pleasing effect for the front and back yoke lines. Cut out paper shapes for pockets, buttons, straps and belt, and experiment with them in different positions. Tuck the crotch under for a more realistic trouser effect. Model the collar in mull or calico (Figures 120–127) or cut flat by either of the two methods shown in Figures 129–132 and 134–139.

Assess the whole appearance of the garment. You could pin a long heavy zip down the centre front to make the pattern look more realistic. Mark all lines lightly with a soft pencil or felt-tipped pen. Take the pattern off the dress form and unpin. Hold ready for later development.

Modelling the collar for the jumpsuit

Step 1

Cut a piece of muslin approximately 25 cm by 30 cm (9¾ in by 12 in). Mark the left edge centre back. Cut away a triangle section 4 cm by 30 cm (1½ in by 12 in), as shown in Figure 120. Pin the newly-cut 'neckline' edge to the suit shell neckline, or dress form, with the centre backs matching. Keeping the bulk of the muslin above the neckline, pin and ease the muslin around the neck to centre front (Figures 121 and 122).

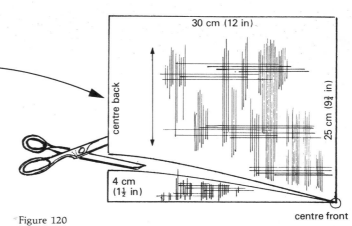

Figure 120

Step 2

Turn down the collar and assess the result. If in doubt continue raising or lowering parts of the collar neckline, thereby causing it to be more or less curved, until the desired degree of roll is achieved. Outline with tape possible collar shapes until the desired shape is established. Mark the outline lightly with dots using a soft pencil or felt-tipped pen. Mark also the centre back, neckline and centre front point.

Figure 121

Figure 122

Figure 123

Figure 124

Step 3
Remove the pattern from the dress form and lay it flat
on the table (Figures 125). True all lightly dotted lines,
paying attention to the right angles at centre back. Place
the centre back of the modelled muslin collar to the fold
of the pattern paper and trace through (Figure 126).
Unfold the paper and draw collar lines on the tracing
wheel marks. This pattern represents the undercollar
(Figure 127(a)). For the top collar allow 5 mm ($\frac{1}{4}$ in)
around the outer edge of the collar from nothing at the
centre front point. Trace through and draft the top
collar adding all relevant information (Figure 127(b)).

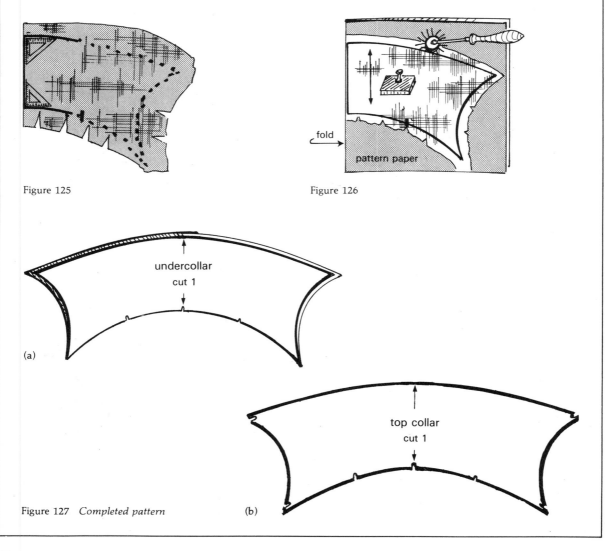

Figure 125

fold

pattern paper

Figure 126

undercollar
cut 1

(a)

top collar
cut 1

Figure 127 *Completed pattern*

(b)

Figure 128

Jumpsuit collar cut flat method 1

Step 1
Outline the upper part of the front pattern. Mark the pivoting point where the shoulder and neck 'fitting' lines intersect (Figure 129).

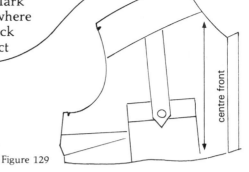

Figure 129

Step 2
Place the back pattern on to the outlined front with pivoting points meeting. Pivot the back shoulder point down until it is 13 cm (5 in) away from the front shoulder point (Figure 130). Outline the back centre line and neckline.

Step 3
Draw the collar shape according to the design and trace off. Allow seam turnings on the outer edge of the collar only. This is the *undercollar* (Figure 132(a)). Develop the *top collar* (Figure 132(b)) as described on page 62, and shown in Figure 127.

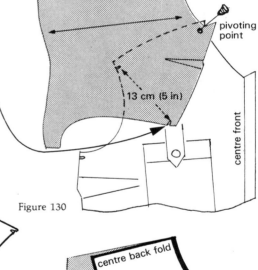

Figure 130

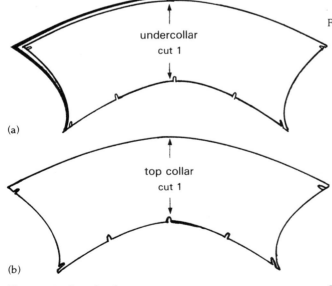

(a)

undercollar
cut 1

top collar
cut 1

(b)

Figure 132 *Completed pattern*

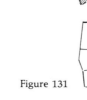

Figure 131

Figure 133

Jumpsuit collar cut flat method 2

Step 1

Outline the upper part of the front pattern. Draw the shape of the collar according to the design as seen from the front (Figure 134). Extend the shoulder line by approximately 25 cm (10 in) as shown in Figure 135.

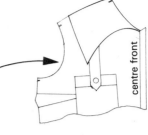

Figure 134

Step 2

Place the back pattern face down with the shoulder-neck points meeting as shown in Figure 136. Drop the back shoulder point 8 cm ($3\frac{1}{4}$ in) below the extended shoulder line. Outline the upper part of the back, especially the back neckline and part of the centre back. Fold the paper under and crease. Trace the collar outline with a tracing wheel (Figure 137).

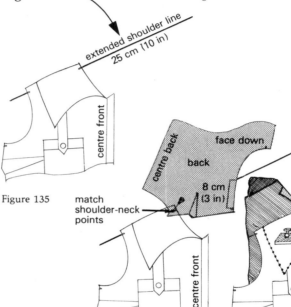

Figure 135

match shoulder-neck points

Figure 136

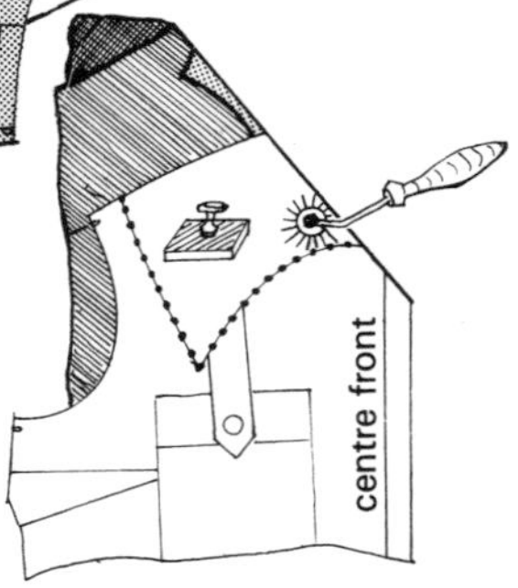

Figure 137

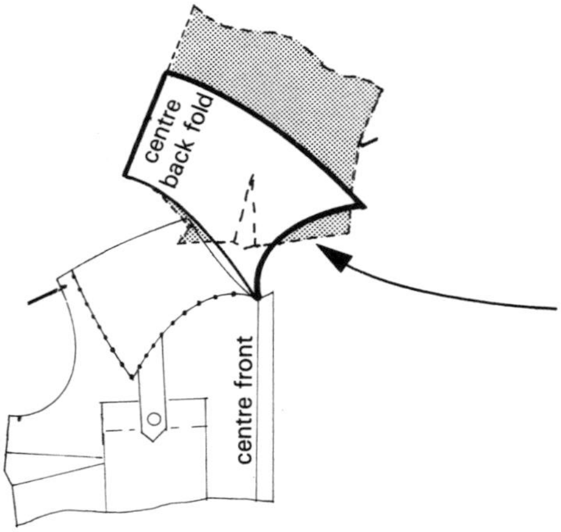

Step 3

Unfold the paper and draw the collar on the tracing wheel marks and extend to centre back (Figure 138). The completed collar pattern is shown in Figure 139.

Figure 138

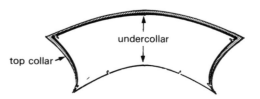

undercollar

top collar

Figure 139 *Completed pattern*

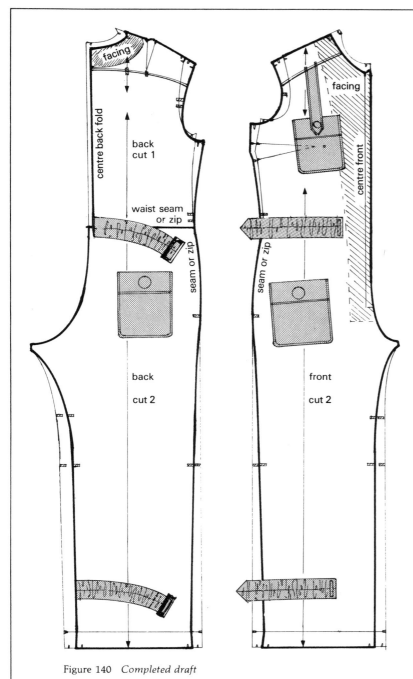

back
cut 1

centre back fold

facing

waist seam
or zip

seam or zip

back

cut 2

front

cut 2

centre front

facing

seam or zip

Figure 140 *Completed draft*

Step 4
Lay the pattern flat on the
table. Perfect and redraw
all pencilled lines, place
balance marks and draw
the facings. Mark on the
pattern the positions of the
belt, straps and pockets.

If preferred, this suit can
be cut without a waist
seam or zip.

Note: The nape to waist
length is longer than the
body measurement to
allow for greater ease of
movement.

Having completed the
draft (Figure 140) keep it
safe for future reference (it
contains all the relevant
information and will be
useful throughout the
making of the pattern).

Step 5

Trace off all the pattern pieces. As the original basic
jumpsuit pattern had seam turnings, only new style
features in this pattern will need seam allowances. Cut
out, preferably in calico, and make the toile for final
proving and adjustments (Figure 141).

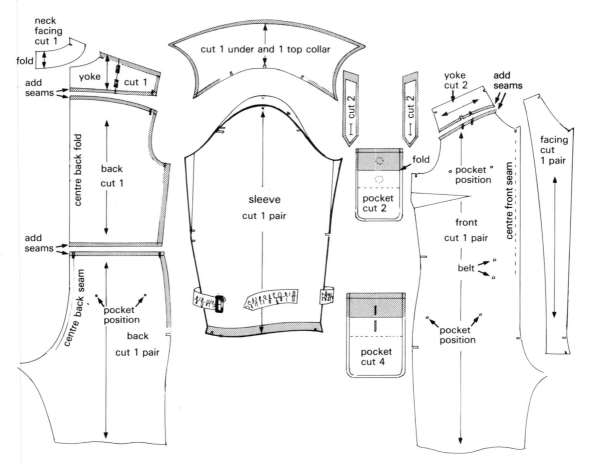

Figure 141 *Completed pattern*

3 Culottes

This sports garment first became fashionable at the beginning of the twentieth century as the 'divided cycling skirt' (Figure 142). The garment hangs loosely and is intended to look like a skirt (Figure 143). Only in movement does the division become apparent. Most skirt shapes, except peg-top skirts, can be used to construct a divided skirt, whether they are straight, circular or pleated, provided that they have a centre front and a centre back seam.

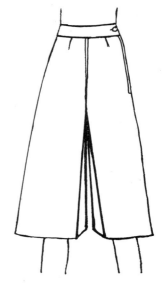

Figure 143

Figure 142   *The 'divided cycling skirt'*

Measurements for the size 12 culottes are:

Hip level   20 cm   (8 in)
Finished hip measurement   99 cm   (39 in)
Crotch level = body rise + ease.
   Body rise 25.5 cm (10 in) + ease
   5 cm (2 in)   30.5 cm   (12 in)

Constructing culottes

Step 1
Draw two parallel lines one quarter of the hip measurement (that is, 25 cm ($9\frac{3}{4}$ in)) away from each other. Mark the left line centre front and the right line centre back. Mark also the hip level position (Figure 144).

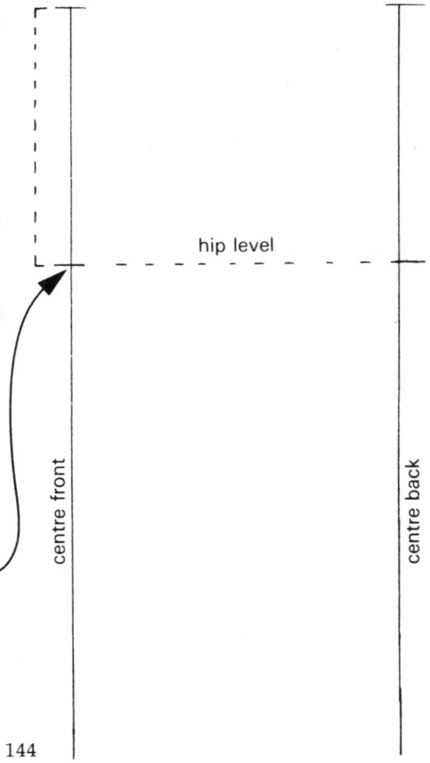

hip level

centre front

centre back

Figure 144

Step 2

Place the *front* and *back skirt blocks* (page 14) to their respective lines, and outline. Draw the crotch level line 30.5 cm (12 in) down from the waist line and remove the blocks (Figure 145).

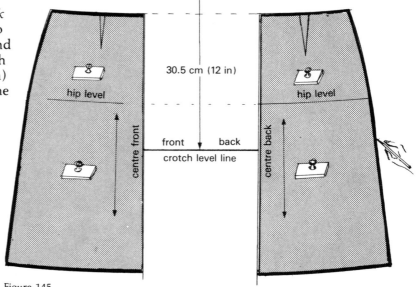

Figure 145

Step 3

On the front section of the crotch line mark half the front hip level line measurement *minus* 2 cm ($\frac{3}{4}$ in), and on the back section of the crotch line mark half the back hip level measurement *plus* 2 cm ($\frac{3}{4}$ in). Square the line down and complete the hem line (Figure 146).

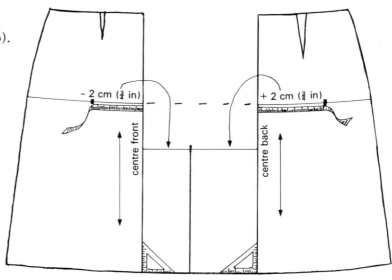

Figure 146

Step 4
Complete the crotch seam curve as shown in Figure 147. Place balance marks to indicate the joining of seams. Add seam allowances, grain line and other relevant information.

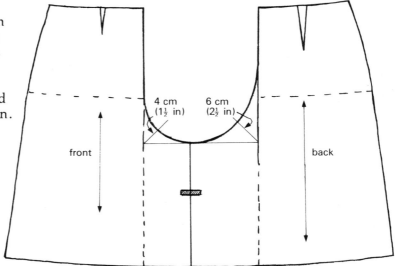

Figure 147

Step 5
When making culottes, assemble one leg at a time. Machine the outside leg seam first, then the inside leg seam. Repeat this procedure for the other leg. Finish by stitching the crotch seam (see Figure 83 on page 42). Leave an opening for the zip where required. Figure 148 shows the completed pattern.

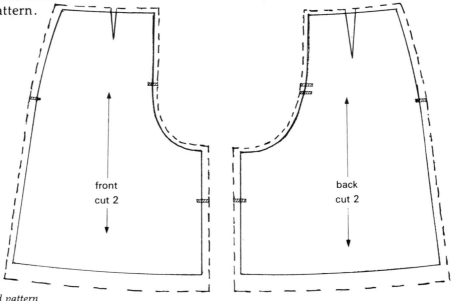

Figure 148 *Completed pattern*

Flared culottes

The appearance of a flare is achieved by increasing the hem circumference and eliminating darts as a means of fitting the waist. This can be achieved by pivoting the culotte pattern (Figure 149). The pivoting point of the culotte front is immediately below the dart point whereas the pivoting point of the culotte back is on the hip level line. By this means it is possible to obtain the same degree of flare in both the back and the front completed patterns.

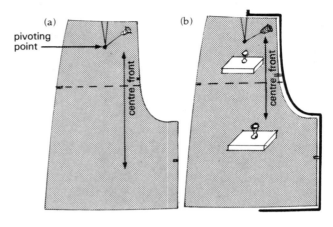

Figure 149

Step 1
Establish the pivoting point. Place the pattern on a sheet of paper and outline the centre front section as shown in Figure 149(a) and (b). Crossmark the position of the inner dart line and the balance marks.

Step 2
With the scriber on the pivoting point, pivot the pattern to the right until the outer dart line meets the previously drawn crossmark. Draw the remaining outline of the culotte. Remove the pattern and complete the draft (Figure 150(a) and (b)).

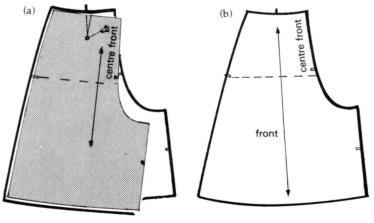

Figure 150

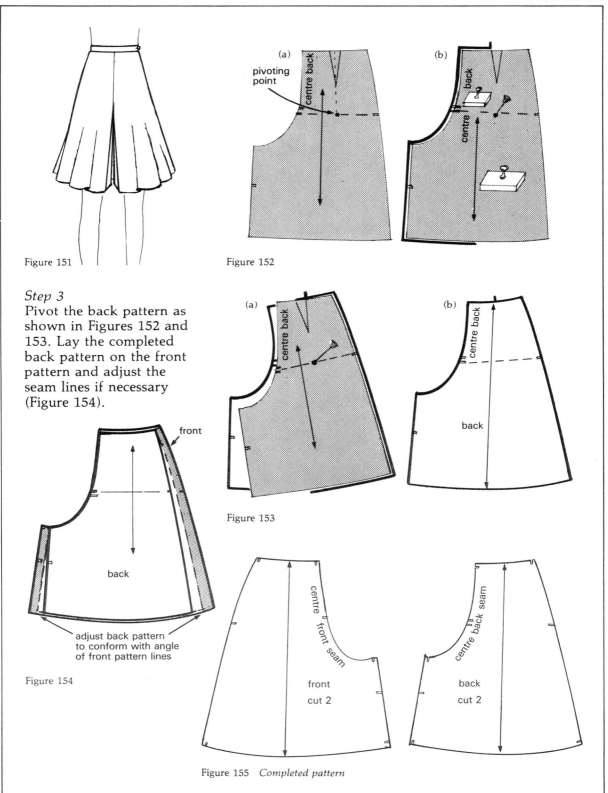

Figure 151

Figure 152

(a) pivoting point — centre back

(b) centre back

Step 3
Pivot the back pattern as shown in Figures 152 and 153. Lay the completed back pattern on the front pattern and adjust the seam lines if necessary (Figure 154).

(a) centre back

(b) centre back — back

Figure 153

front

back

adjust back pattern to conform with angle of front pattern lines

Figure 154

centre front seam

front
cut 2

centre back seam

back
cut 2

Figure 155 *Completed pattern*

Culottes with inverted pleats (Figure 156)

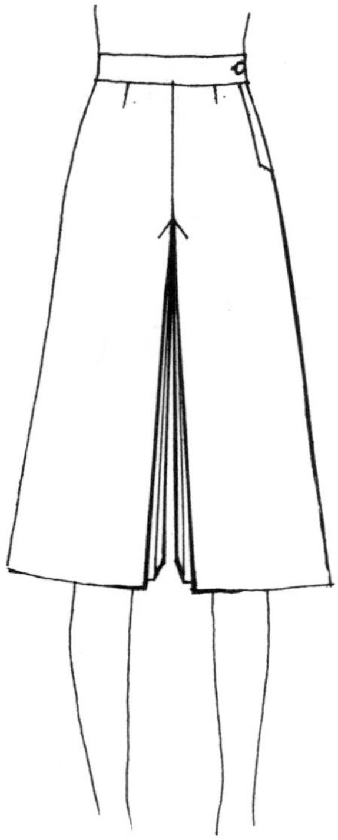

Step 1

Outline the *straight skirt block* 26 cm (10¼ in) away from the edge of the paper (Figure 157). Draw a line for the inverted pleat at a distance of 10 cm (4 in) from the centre front and parallel to it.

Figure 156

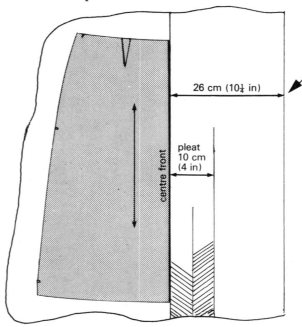

26 cm (10¼ in)

centre front

pleat
10 cm
(4 in)

Figure 157

Step 2

Fold and crease the inverted pleat (Figure 158) and join the inside leg section to the centre front (Figure 159).

Figure 160 shows the completed pattern with the inverted pleat extending to the waist line.

Step 3

If the inside pleat allowance is folded towards the centre front (Figure 161) and the superfluous paper cut away, an open seam will result. This, when pressed open, will be less bulky at the waist (Figure 162). Fold back the inside pleat to its original inverted pleat position and when the culotte is made up, stitch the pleat in position.

Repeat this procedure for the development of the culotte back.

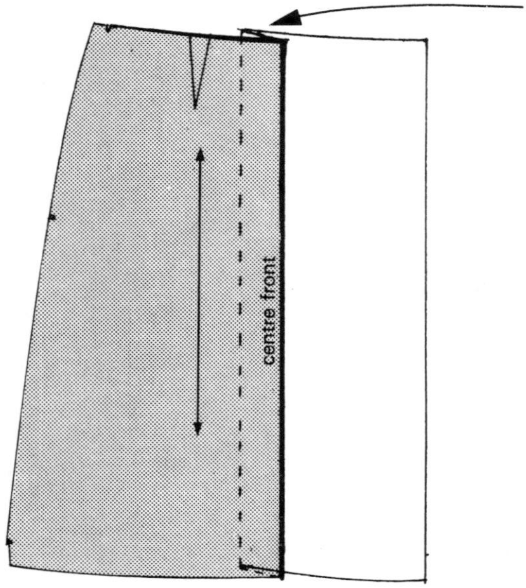

centre front

Figure 158

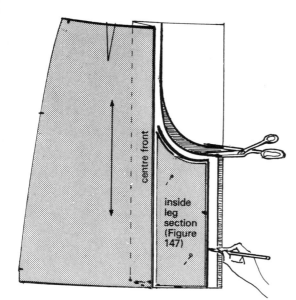

Figure 159

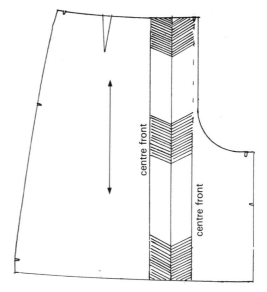

Figure 160   *Completed pattern*

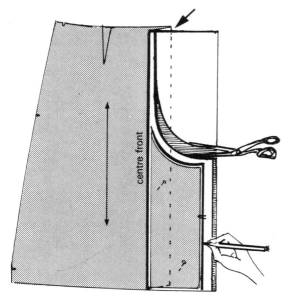

Figure 161

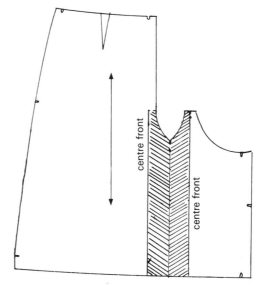

Figure 162   *Completed pattern*

Various culotte styles

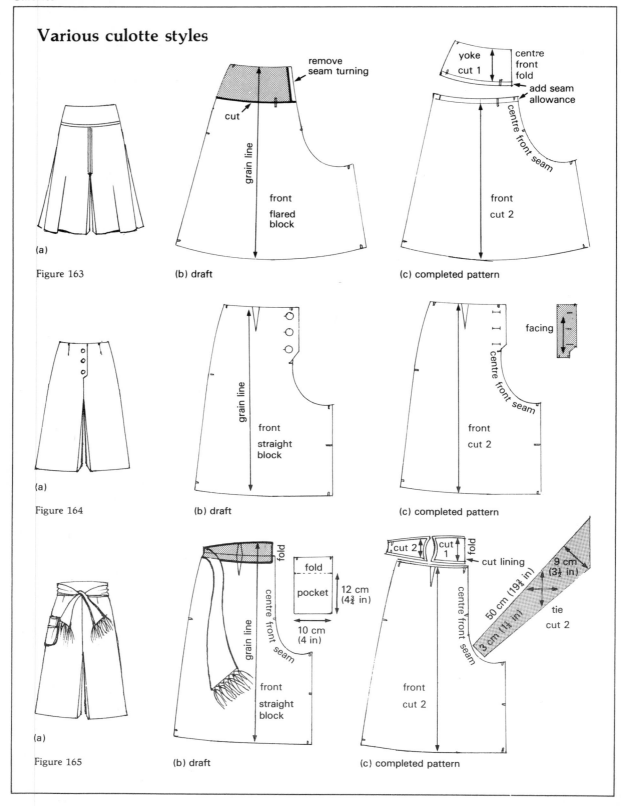

Figure 163

(a)

(b) draft — remove seam turning / cut / grain line / front flared block

(c) completed pattern — yoke cut 1 / centre front fold / add seam allowance / centre front seam / front cut 2

Figure 164

(a)

(b) draft — grain line / front straight block

(c) completed pattern — facing / centre front seam / front cut 2

Figure 165

(a)

(b) draft — fold / centre front seam / grain line / front straight block / fold / pocket / 12 cm (4¾ in) / 10 cm (4 in)

(c) completed pattern — cut 2 / cut 1 / fold / cut lining / centre front seam / front cut 2 / 9 cm (3½ in) / 50 cm (19¾ in) / 3 cm (1¼ in) / tie cut 2

Long half-circle culottes cut flat

Measurements for size 12 are:

| Waist | 64 cm (25 in) |
| Length | 100 cm (39½ in) |

Method of construction
Subtract 2.5 cm (1 in) from the waist measurement (64 – 2.5 = 61.5 cm). One third of this measurement is the radius for drafting the waist line, that is:

61.5 cm (24 in) ÷ 3 = 20.5 cm (8 in)

See also Chapter 11 of *Modelling and Flat Cutting for Fashion 1.*

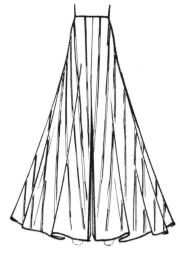

Figure 166　*Front view*

Figure 167　*Back view*

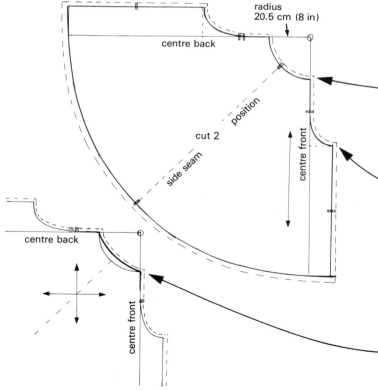

Figure 168

Step 1
Referring to Figure 168, square out from point O. Draw a quarter-circle for the waist line, with a radius of 20.5 cm (8 in). Measure the desired length from the waist line and draft the hem line. Lower the crotch level to 33 cm (13 in) for a loose fit and add the inside leg section as for standard culottes (Figure 148). Add the balance marks, grain line and seam allowances.

Experiment with the waist line on the dress form or figure. A shallower line will sometimes achieve a smoother fit with the fulness more evenly distributed all around.

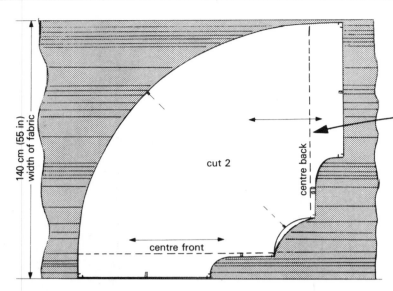

Step 2
Fabric of at least 140 cm (55 in) in width is required for half-circle culottes without side seams. Note the grain line (Figure 169). The centre back is on the weft grain and the centre front on the warp. This can be reversed if desired. The side seam position can be placed on the straight grain, but much wider fabric would be required and, therefore, a seam is more appropriate here.

Figure 169

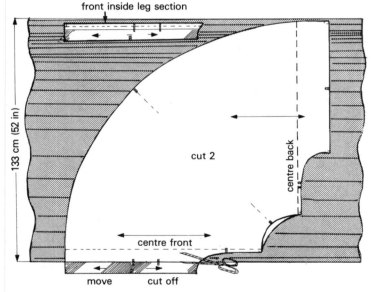

Step 3
If the width of the fabric is less than 140 cm, in this instance 133 cm (52 in), part of the inside leg pattern section is cut away, seam turnings allowed for and the cut-out section joined by a seam to the main body of the garment (Figure 170).

Figure 170

Culottes in narrower fabric width

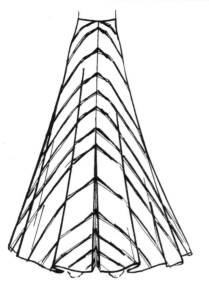

Figure 171   *Front view*

Figure 172   *Side view*

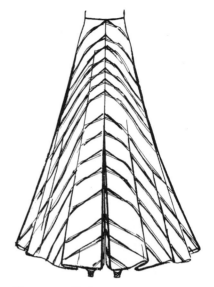

Figure 173   *Back view*

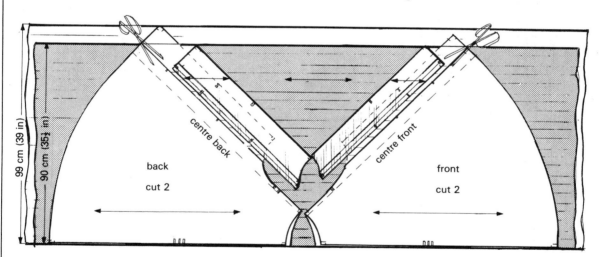

Figure 174

The culottes shown in Figures 171–173 are cut on a different grain from those shown in Figure 166. This pair has side seams and so a narrower fabric width can be used. A further reduction in width is possible by cutting parts of both inside leg sections separately (Figure 174).

Interesting effects with striped and checked fabrics can be achieved by changing the grain of the material on which the pattern is placed.

Four-gored half-circle culottes

For this style, the pattern is placed on the fabric with the straight grain running down the centre of back and front sections. The finished skirt hangs well and is evenly balanced all around. Mitred effects are obtained on all seams if striped or checked fabric is used.

The lay shown in Figure 178 is for two different widths of material. Compare the length of the fabric.

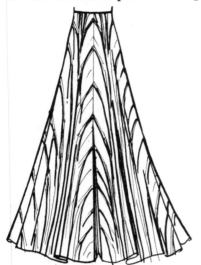

Figure 175   *Front view*

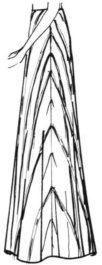

Figure 176   *Side view*

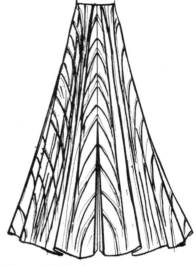

Figure 177   *Back view*

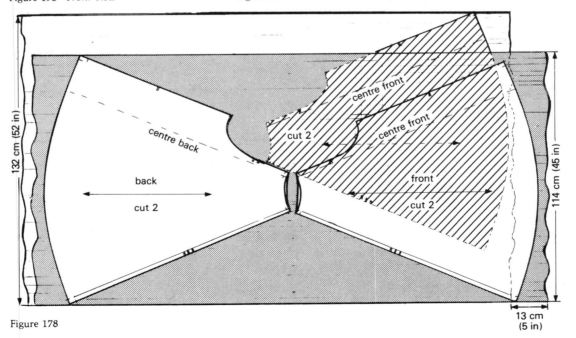

Figure 178

4 Shorts and stretch fabric pants

The cut of shorts is influenced primarily by the function for which they are intended. This will determine whether the shorts are to be loose-fitting or figure-hugging, and whether the fabric selected is woven or knitted.

Shorts are in fact trousers or culottes cut short, and a designer must select the correct basic block which, when used to develop the final pattern, promises to obtain the desired fitting qualities. For example, the shorts shown in Figure 179 are developed from the basic skirt block (page 14); Figure 180 from the basic culottes pattern (Figure 148); Figure 181 from the straight trouser block (page 15 or page 37) and Figure 182 from the jeans pattern (Figure 90).

The many names used to describe particular kinds of shorts vary with the language of fashion of the time, and instantly bring to mind the fashion features associated with them. Thus, there are, or were, clam-diggers, pedal-pushers, Bermudas, gauchos and trunks, pants and, of course, plain and pleated shorts.

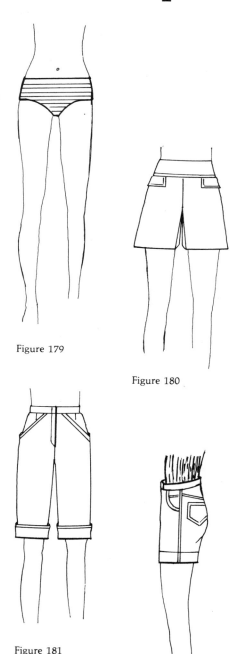

Figure 179

Figure 180

Figure 181

Figure 182

Short pants in knitted stretch fabric
(Figure 183)

The length and girth measurements of the pattern must be reduced to less than the body measurements, depending on the stretchability of the fabric that is to be used. Test the fabric beforehand. In this case 6 cm (2½ in) are subtacted from the standard size 12 body measurements.

No ease allowed for body rise   25.5 cm (10 in)
Length of pants from waist   29   cm (11½ in)

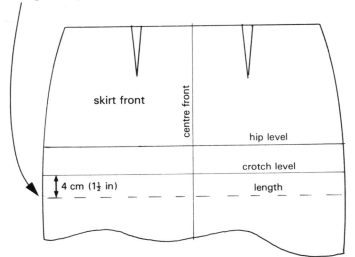

Figure 184

Figure 183

Step 1
Outline the full front of the *straight skirt block* (page 14) as shown in Figure 184. Measure body rise on the centre front line and draw the crotch level line.

Step 2
Reduce the side seams by the amount of ease allowed on the skirt block plus the reduction for stretch fabric. Shape the front and back leg lengths and gusset, as shown in Figure 185. Allow seam turnings.

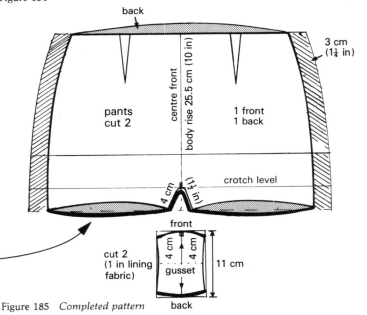

Figure 185   *Completed pattern*

Hipster trunks in knitted stretch fabric
(Figure 186)

Proceed as for the short pants (see Figure 183). Lower the waist level by the desired amount and shape the front and back leg lengths according to the design. Add seam allowances as required, according to the type of seam neatening that is to be used. Mark the grain line. Figure 187 shows the completed pattern.

Figure 186

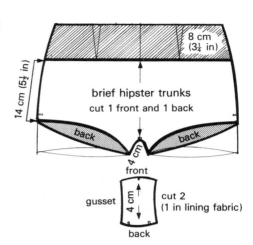

8 cm
(3¼ in)

14 cm (5½ in)

brief hipster trunks
cut 1 front and 1 back

back   back

4 cm

front

gusset   4 cm   cut 2
(1 in lining fabric)

back

Figure 187   *Completed pattern*

For Bermuda pants (Figure 188), lower the waist level and lengthen the legs. Note the gusset to correspond with the longer leg. Add seam turnings, balance marks and grain line (Figure 189).

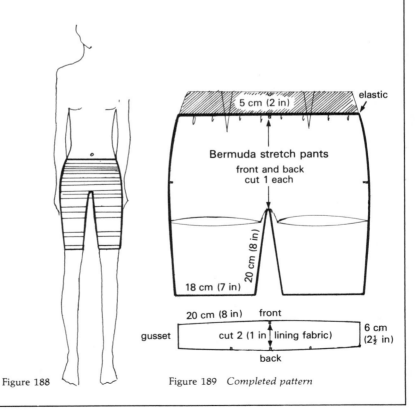

Figure 188

5 cm (2 in)   elastic

Bermuda stretch pants
front and back
cut 1 each

20 cm (8 in)

18 cm (7 in)

20 cm (8 in)   front

gusset   cut 2 (1 in lining fabric)   6 cm
(2½ in)

back

Figure 189   *Completed pattern*

5 Lingerie panties

Step 1
Use the *skirt blocks* shown on page 14 for the development of these panties.

Draw a large T as shown in Figure 191. The horizontal line is equivalent to half the skirt hip measurement. On this line mark one quarter of the hip measurement on each side of the vertical line. Name these points B (back) and F (front).

Step 2
Place the back and front skirt blocks to points B and F, and outline. (The centre back and centre front lines will swing slightly outward by the small amount of flare that was added to the straight skirt side seam.)

Ignore darts and original side seam outlines to hip level. Draw in the new and slightly curved waist and hip lines.

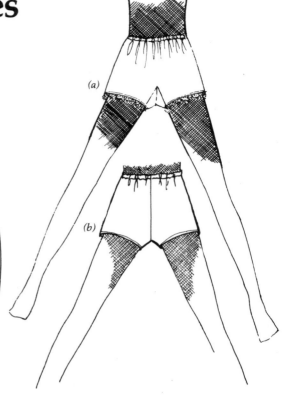

Figure 190

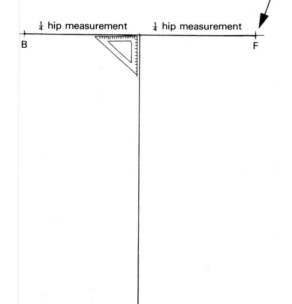

¼ hip measurement   ¼ hip measurement

B   F

Figure 191

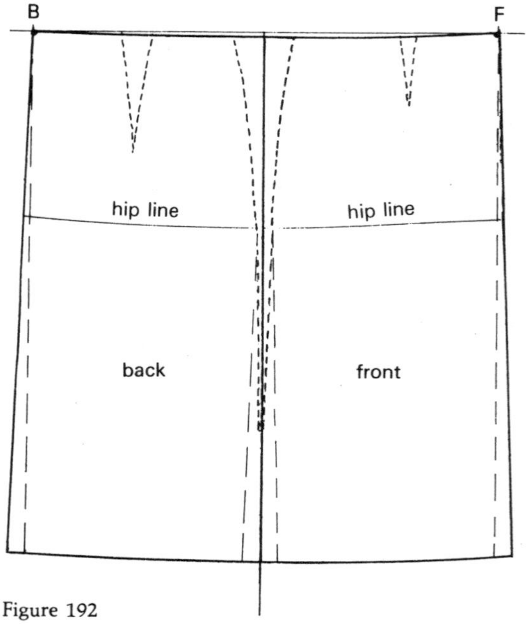

B   F

hip line   hip line

back   front

Figure 192

Step 3

Draw the crotch level line 33 cm (13 in) below and parallel to the waist line. The basic body rise measurement for size 12 is 28–28.5 cm (11–11¼ in) (see Table 2 on page 33). To this measurement add 4.5–5 cm (1¾–2 in) for each size. Extend the crotch level line to the left and right beyond the centre back and centre front lines by 7.5 cm (3 in) and mark intersections B^1 and F^1.

Square down 5 cm (2 in) and draw the hem line parallel to the crotch level line.

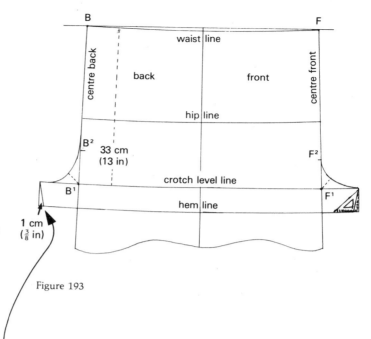

Figure 193

Reduce the inside leg by 1 cm (⅜ in). Draw 3 cm (1¾ in) diagonal lines from B^1 and F^1 as shown in Figure 193. On the centre front line, from F^1, measure up 6 cm (2⅜ in) and mark F^2; on the centre back line, from B^1, measure 7 cm (2¾ in) and mark B^2. Curve the crotch as shown in Figure 193. This is the basic panties block draft.

Step 4

Draw the whole draft again and trace the *back only* on to firm card. Cut out and place over the back block draft. Pivot down by 3 cm (1¼ in) from pivoting point P. Outline from below B^2 around the hem line to meet the front hem line. This gives additional length to the back of the panties and effects a closer fit around the back hem line. This block can be used as it is for panties with a centre front and centre back seam.

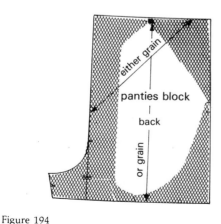

Figure 194

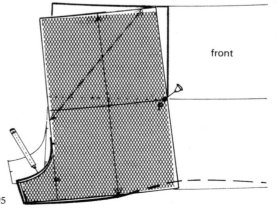

Figure 195

Step 5

Lower the front waist line by 1.5 cm ($\frac{5}{8}$ in) as shown in Figure 196.

An improved fit is achieved in the inside leg area by tightening the gusset seams.

Measure 1.5 cm ($\frac{5}{8}$ in) towards the main body of the panties and draw the gusset seam line as shown. Place balance marks.

Cut off back and front gusset sections and join as shown in Figure 196.

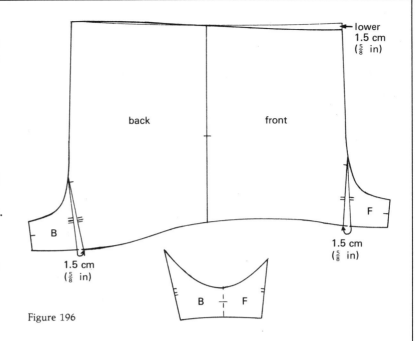

Figure 196

Step 6

Add seam allowances around the gusset and around the panties back and front, except where the inner leg is joined to the gusset, where a seam allowance is 'taken away' rather than added as in the usual way (Figure 197). Try out in a trial fabric and improve the fit if necessary.

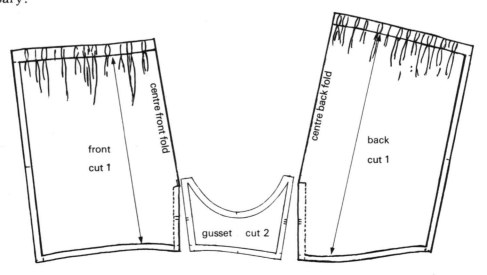

Figure 197   *Completed pattern*

Panties and gusset styles

Note the different lengths of the side seams in each of
the styles in relation to the leg circumference
measurements which are the same in Figures 198–201.
The shape of the gussets is also affected.

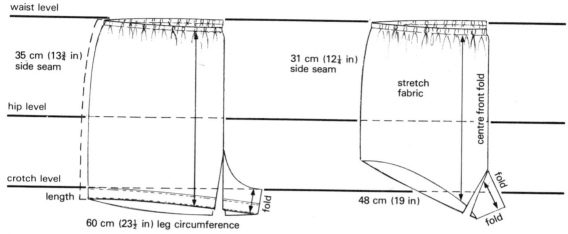

Figure 198

Figure 199

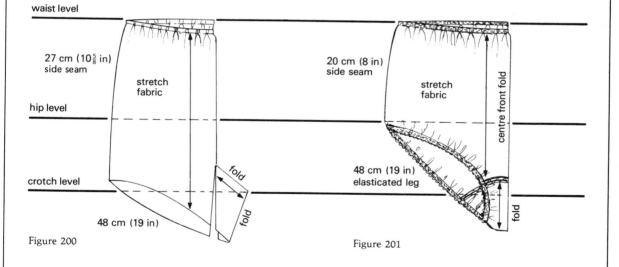

Figure 200

Figure 201

6 Cami-knickers

Cami-knickers based on the panties block

The development of these cami-knickers is based on combining the *basic mini-slip* (given in Chapter 5 of *Modelling and Flat Cutting for Fashion 2*) with the *basic panties block* (Figure 197).

The design shown in Figure 202(a) is cut with centre seams in one part with the gusset, and requires more fabric than the style shown in Figure 202(b) which has separately cut gussets.

The design shown in Figure 202(b) is used most in wholesale production, because it affords the most economical lay with a consequent saving of fabric, and gives additional strength to the gusset point. A weak point would be created in the garment assembly if gussets were inserted into single-layer fabric (as in Figure 203(a)) and more assembly time and skill would also be required.

Figure 202

(a)

(b)

Figure 203   (a)

(b)

front gusset

Finished measurements for size 12 cami-knickers are:
Centre back length $\qquad$ 54 cm ($21\frac{1}{4}$ in)
Underarm circumference $\qquad$ 90 cm ($35\frac{1}{2}$ in)
Hem circumference (excluding gusset) $\qquad$ 168 cm ($66\frac{1}{4}$ in)
Crotch depth* $\qquad$ 34 cm ($13\frac{1}{2}$ in)

Step 1
Outline the *mini-slip block* (Chapter 5 of
Modelling and Flat Cutting for Fashion 2).

Step 2
Raise the hem line by 8 cm (3 in).

Step 3
Add 10 cm (4 in) to the side seams at
hem level and draw new side seam lines
to waist level.

Step 4
Draw style lines, for
example, *midriff*.

Step 5
From waist level draw the
new centre front and back
lines allowing 2 cm ($\frac{3}{4}$ in)
spring at hem line.

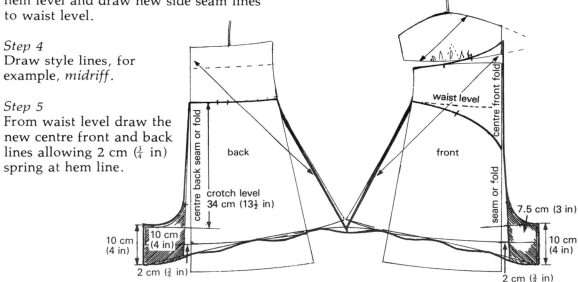

Figure 204 $\qquad$ Figure 205

Step 6
Measure the crotch depth from waist level and square
out as shown. Square down 10 cm (4 in). This line
becomes the button-fastening section and requires a
button extension (see Figures 203(b)–206).

Complete the draft and trace off all pattern parts. Make
a toile to 'prove' the pattern and complete the final
corrected pattern.

*Cami-knickers require an even lower crotch level than
lingerie panties (see page 83 which gives details of body rise
measurements) because of their one-piece construction and
greater strain in the crotch area. The *back gusset* must be
longer to ensure a comfortable button-fastening position.

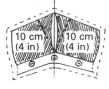

development of
back gusset

Figure 206

7 Maternity wear

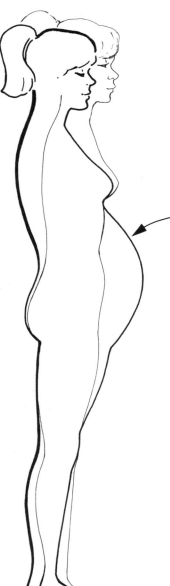

Abdominal expansion in pregnancy varies considerably. It is dependent on a number of physiological changes occurring throughout the nine months of pregnancy and these changes are further individually conditioned. On average, an increase of 18–26 cm (7–10 in) around the waist can be expected (Figure 207).

Garments must be cut wider, particularly in the centre front area, by at least the amount stated above, and cut longer in the front by 5–10 cm (2–4 in) due to abdominal expansion which tends to raise the front hem line of a garment (Figures 208 and 209).

The bust circumference is expected to increase 5–7.5 cm (2–3 in).

Maternity garments are sized so that pregnant women can continue to wear their customary sizes, but patterns are based on the block patterns and dress forms that are one size larger than normal.

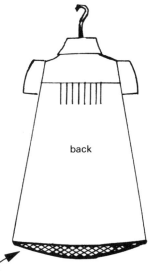

back

Figure 208

Figure 209

Figure 207

A designer should consider the following points when designing maternity garments.

1 Divert attention away from the mid-section of the figure.
2 Aim at suspending fulness from the bust level to balance abdominal protrusion.
3 Emphasize rather than disguise any slim parts of the figure, for example, thigh region, legs and arms (Figures 210–216).

Figure 210

Figure 211

Figure 212

Figure 215 (b)

(a)

Figure 213

Figure 214

Figure 216

Modelling or flat cutting?

It is not essential to model maternity garments on a
dress form. Changes in front length, and adjustments
for ease and comfort can be made on the block patterns
which are used to develop the desired styles.

However, for the designer and cutter who is as yet
inexperienced in the designing and cutting of maternity
garments, modelling and seeing the toile of a planned
garment on a padded dress form, or better still, on a
pregnant figure, is a most valuable experience. It enables
the designer-cutter to note at once the effect, pleasing or
otherwise, of the distribution of fulness on the figure
and the most flattering placements of seams, yokes,
pockets and buttons. Stripes, checks and other
prominent fabric patterns can be indicated in pencil or
felt-tipped pen on the toile material; the possible use of
decorative trimmings can be assessed visually by
experimentation until the designer is satisfied with the
final look.

The knowledge and understanding acquired by working
on a three-dimensional form can then be applied when
constructing maternity wear patterns by the flat cutting
method.

Method of padding a dress form for maternity wear*

The dress form should be one size larger than the normal size.

Step 1

Model first one half of a corset-type foundation in firm cotton fabric, such as unbleached calico, to fit the dress form. The bra section should be cut on the bias of the fabric. Shape the centre front and princess line seams and allow an extension at centre back for a tape fastening (Figure 217). Mark the bust and waist line with tailor's chalk.

Step 2

When satisfied with the fit, mark all seams and the small underbust dart carefully. Use the modelled shapes to cut out the other side of the foundation, sew up and press most seams open. Pin the foundation to the dress form with pressed raw edge seams facing outward (Figure 218).

Step 3

For the padding, prepare the plastic foam shoulder pads which are to be used whole or sliced into wedge-shaped sections, and also washable polyester wadding. This type of wadding can cause skin irritations in some people and, therefore, it is wise to wear gloves when working with the wadding.

Figure 217

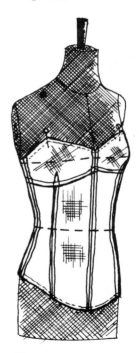

Figure 218

*The author wishes to acknowledge the valuable suggestions made by Barrie H. Lancaster.

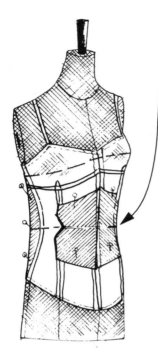

Figure 219

Step 4

Pin, tack and sew the four cut-to-shape plastic foam pads to the stomach area as shown in Figure 219. Secure wedge-shaped slices of foam pad to the side seams, centre back and princess line seam (Figure 220). Sew to the foundation garment only and not to the dress form! For this, a curved upholstery needle is very helpful. Now pin, tack and sew layers of the washable wadding over the foam pads and the bust area as shown in Figure 221. Aim for a smooth graduated effect and mark the bust and waist line on each successive layer of wadding as you go along. Measure the circumference from time to time as padding is added, until the desired increase has been achieved. Then, because the final calico covering tends to compress the wadding, add a little more padding as a precaution.

Model the now differently shaped outer cover over the padding. Pin the seams in harmony with the new body shape, continuous with the seams of the dress form. Machine seams, attach tapes to centre back, 'bag out' to neaten all edges and secure to the dress form for further use (Figure 222).

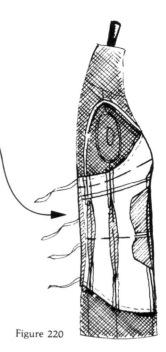

Figure 220

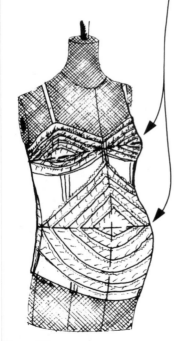

Figure 221

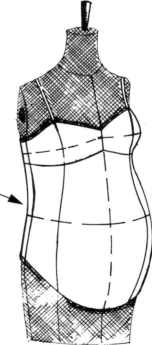

Figure 222

Development 1 of the maternity dress block

The *A-line dress block* is prerequisite to the development of the *maternity dress block*. (The A-line dress block is covered in Chapter 3 of *Modelling and Flat Cutting for Fashion 1*.)

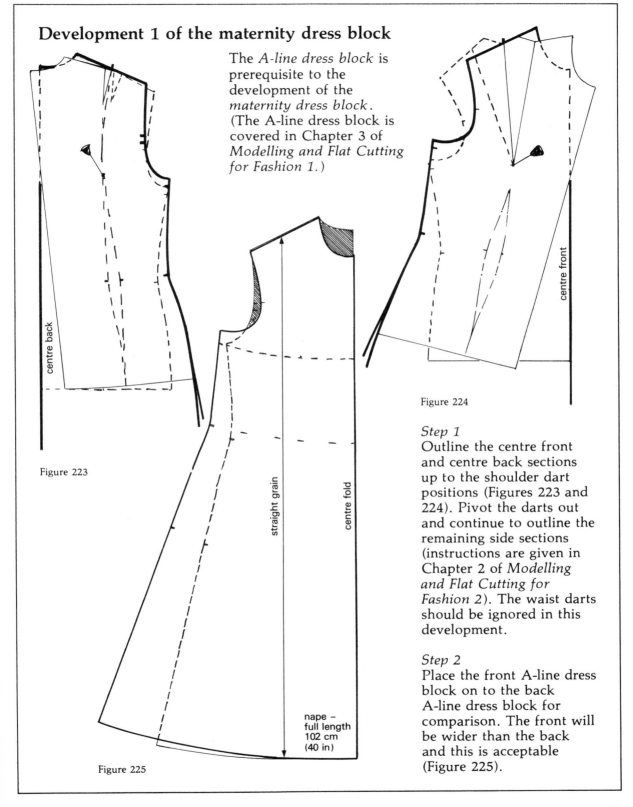

Figure 223

Figure 224

Figure 225

centre back

centre front

straight grain

centre fold

nape – full length 102 cm (40 in)

Step 1
Outline the centre front and centre back sections up to the shoulder dart positions (Figures 223 and 224). Pivot the darts out and continue to outline the remaining side sections (instructions are given in Chapter 2 of *Modelling and Flat Cutting for Fashion 2*). The waist darts should be ignored in this development.

Step 2
Place the front A-line dress block on to the back A-line dress block for comparison. The front will be wider than the back and this is acceptable (Figure 225).

93

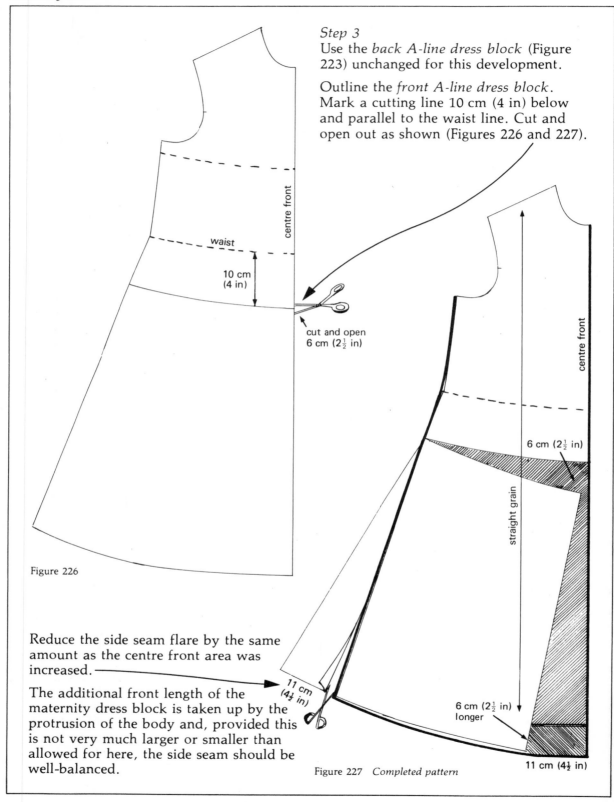

Step 3

Use the *back A-line dress block* (Figure 223) unchanged for this development.

Outline the *front A-line dress block*. Mark a cutting line 10 cm (4 in) below and parallel to the waist line. Cut and open out as shown (Figures 226 and 227).

centre front

waist

10 cm (4 in)

cut and open
6 cm (2½ in)

Figure 226

6 cm (2½ in)

straight grain

centre front

6 cm (2½ in)
longer

Reduce the side seam flare by the same amount as the centre front area was increased.

11 cm (4½ in)

The additional front length of the maternity dress block is taken up by the protrusion of the body and, provided this is not very much larger or smaller than allowed for here, the side seam should be well-balanced.

11 cm (4½ in)

Figure 227 *Completed pattern*

Development 2 of the maternity dress block

The maternity dress block shown in Figure 227, with its accompanying back block (Figure 233), produces a definite A-line silhouette. If a straighter side seam is preferred, use Development 2, which is outlined below. In order to compare the fit and hang of the two maternity blocks, cut each block in paper (allowing for seam turnings) and pin together. Try on a padded dress form or pregnant figure and note the difference. Then determine which of the blocks is more suitable as a basis for the development of the style in question.

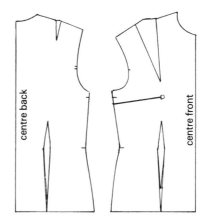

Figure 228

Step 1
Use the *back* and *front hip blocks* (on page 13), but one size larger. (See also Chapter 3 and Chapter 9 of *Modelling and Flat Cutting for Fashion 1*.) Mark the desired position of the underarm dart on the front hip block.

Step 2
Place the front hip block on the pattern paper. Outline the centre front section from the shoulder dart to the underarm dart mark (Figure 229(a)).

Pivot the block to the right until the left arm of the shoulder dart overlaps the right arm (Figure 229(b). Outline as shown.

Remove the block and complete the underarm dart (Figure 229(c)).

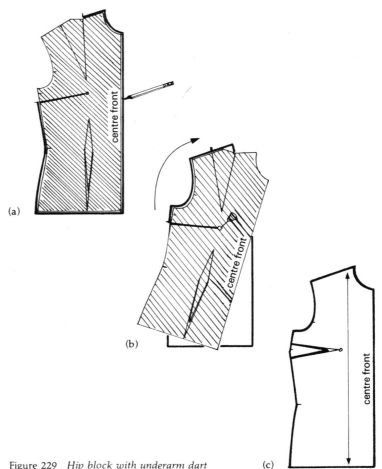

(a)

(b)

(c)

Figure 229 *Hip block with underarm dart*

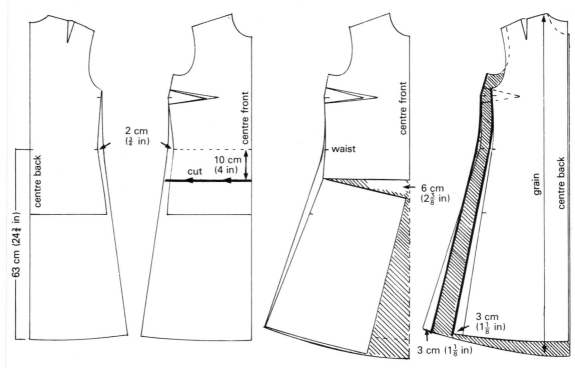

Figure 230   Figure 231   Figure 232   Figure 233

Step 3
Outline the back hip block (Figure 230). Increase the waist by 2 cm ($\frac{3}{4}$ in) and lengthen as shown.

Step 4
Outline the front hip block. Repeat as for the back. Cut on the line 10 cm (4 in) below the waist (Figure 231).

Step 5
Open the slash 6 cm ($2\frac{3}{8}$ in). Outline and blend the side seam from the waist to the hem line as shown in Figure 232.

Step 6
Outline the new front (Figure 232). Place the back (Figure 230) face down on the outlined front and outline. Reduce the front and increase the back side seams at hem level by 3 cm ($1\frac{1}{8}$ in) (Figure 233).

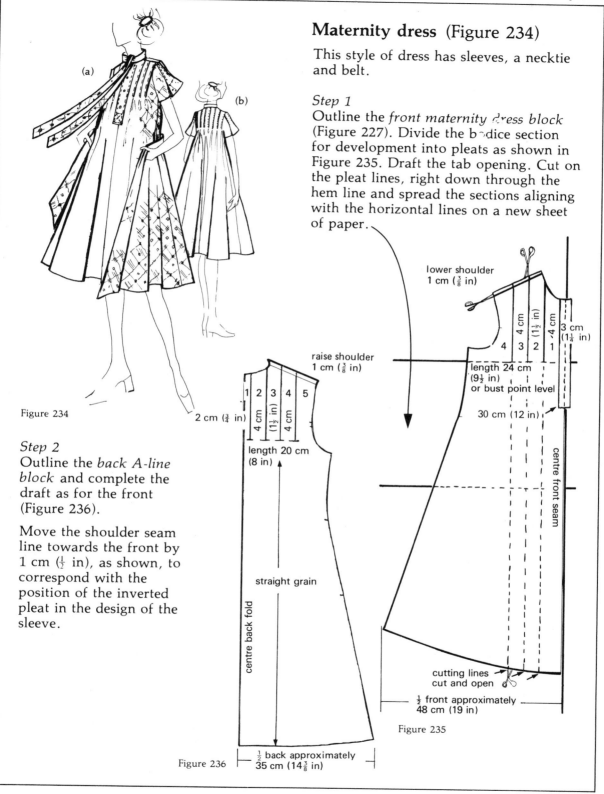

Figure 234

Maternity dress (Figure 234)

This style of dress has sleeves, a necktie and belt.

Step 1
Outline the *front maternity dress block* (Figure 227). Divide the bodice section for development into pleats as shown in Figure 235. Draft the tab opening. Cut on the pleat lines, right down through the hem line and spread the sections aligning with the horizontal lines on a new sheet of paper.

Step 2
Outline the *back A-line block* and complete the draft as for the front (Figure 236).

Move the shoulder seam line towards the front by 1 cm ($\frac{1}{2}$ in), as shown, to correspond with the position of the inverted pleat in the design of the sleeve.

lower shoulder
1 cm ($\frac{3}{8}$ in)

4 cm ($1\frac{1}{2}$ in)

3 cm ($1\frac{1}{4}$ in)

length 24 cm ($9\frac{1}{2}$ in) or bust point level

30 cm (12 in)

centre front seam

cutting lines cut and open

$\frac{1}{2}$ front approximately 48 cm (19 in)

Figure 235

raise shoulder
1 cm ($\frac{3}{8}$ in)

2 cm ($\frac{3}{4}$ in)

4 cm ($1\frac{1}{2}$ in)

length 20 cm (8 in)

straight grain

centre back fold

Figure 236

$\frac{1}{2}$ back approximately 35 cm ($14\frac{3}{8}$ in)

Step 3
Complete the front pattern as shown in Figure 237, adding seam allowances, grain line and other relevant information. Develop the back dress pattern in the same manner.

For the tab fastening, cut two pieces, as one piece is applied as facing for the underside of the opening.

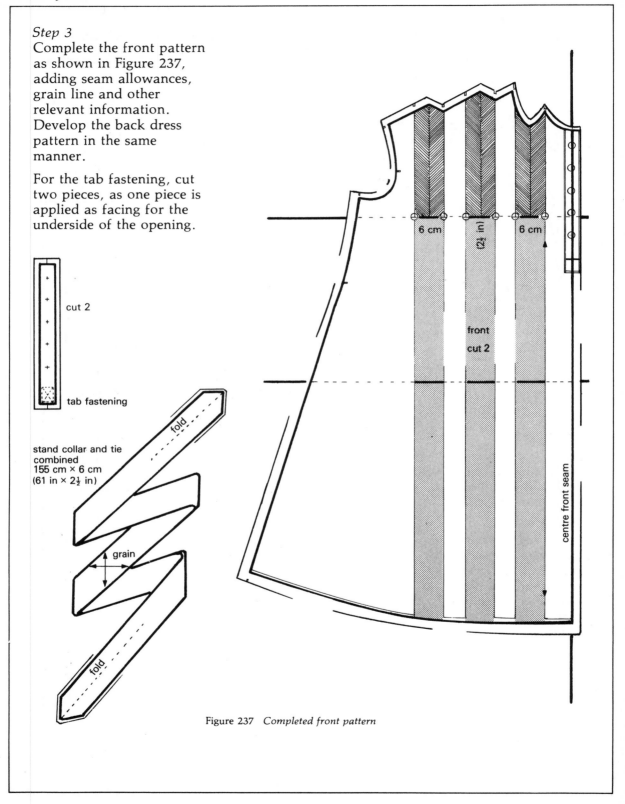

cut 2

tab fastening

stand collar and tie combined
155 cm × 6 cm
(61 in × 2½ in)

grain

fold

fold

6 cm

(2½ in)

6 cm

front
cut 2

centre front seam

Figure 237 *Completed front pattern*

Alternative method of development

By using this alternative and quicker track-drafting method, the same final pattern (Figure 237) can be obtained. The method obviates cutting up the pleat lines and separating the pattern sections.

It is important that the three pleat lines, the horizontal bust line and the hip line are drawn on the *maternity dress block*.

Step 1
On pattern paper draw a horizontal line 30 cm (12 in) longer than the length from the shoulder to hem line. Square up two lines to correspond with the hip line and bust line on the block pattern (Figure 238).

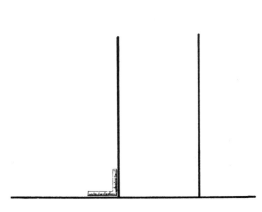

Figure 238

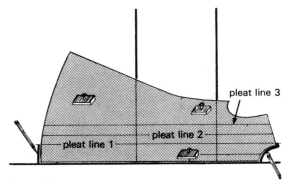

Figure 239

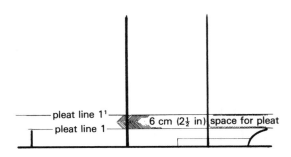

Figure 240

Step 2
Place the dress block on the horizontal guide line. Align hip and bust lines with the guide lines on the paper. Outline the neck and part of the hem line to pleat line 1 (Figure 239).

Step 3
Remove the block pattern and draw pleat line 1. Leave 6 cm (2½ in) space for pleat allowance and draw pleat line 1' (Figure 240).

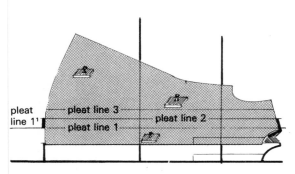

Figure 241

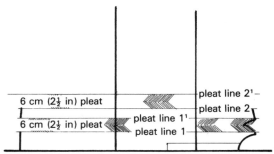

Figure 242

Step 4

Move the dress block forward, aligning pleat line 1 with pleat line 1^1 on the pattern paper. Outline as shown in Figure 241.

Step 5

Remove the dress block and draw pleat line 2. Allow 6 cm (2½ in) for the pleat, and draw pleat line 2^1 (Figure 242).

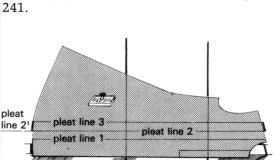

Figure 243

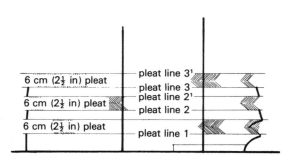

Figure 244

Step 6

Move the dress block forward and align pleat line 2 with pleat line 2^1. Outline as shown in Figure 243.

Step 7

Remove the block and draw pleat line 3. Allow 6 cm (2½ in) for the pleat and draw pleat line 3^1 (Figure 244).

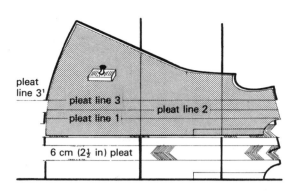

Figure 245

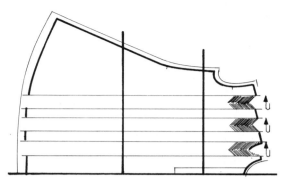

Figure 246

Step 8
Move the dress block forward. Align pleat line 3 with pleat line 3^1. Outline as shown in Figure 245.

Step 9
Remove the block and add seam turnings where possible (Figure 246). Cut out (see Figure 247).

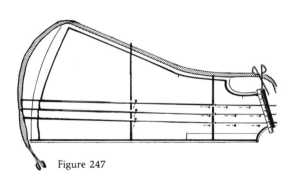

Figure 247

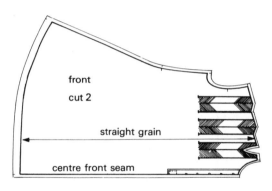

Figure 248   *Completed pattern*

Step 10
Fold pleats and pin. Draw the improved shoulder line. Add seam allowances and cut (Figure 247).

Figure 248 shows the completed pattern.

Pleated sleeves for the maternity dress (Figure 249)

Figure 249

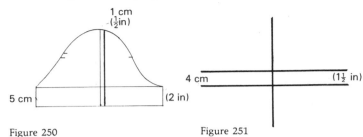

Figure 250

Figure 251

Step 1
Move the centre of the sleeve 1 cm ($\frac{3}{8}$ in) towards the front (Figure 250).

Draw a cross with horizontal lines spaced as shown in Figure 251.

Place the sleeve on the cross (Figure 252).

Step 2
Pivot to the left, touching line, and outline as shown in Figure 253.

Pivot to the right, touching line, and outline as shown in Figure 254.

Figure 255 shows the sleeve shape as used for development.

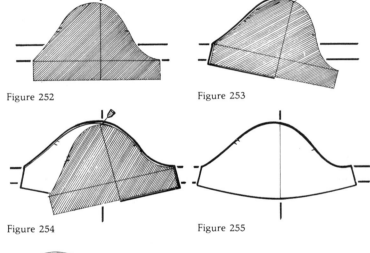

Figure 252

Figure 253

Figure 254

Figure 255

Step 3
Divide into sections, separate for pleats as shown (Figures 256 and 257).

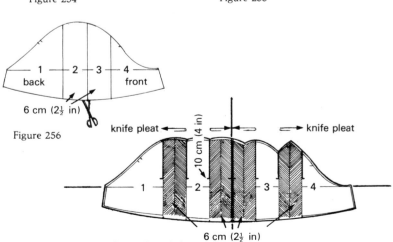

Figure 256

Figure 257 *Completed pleated sleeve*

Figure 258

Maternity smock or jacket

The *maternity dress block* (Figure 227) is used in the development of a variety of garments.

The garments shown in Figures 258 and 259 are similar. One is made of light-weight fabric and can be worn in place of a blouse. It is developed from the maternity dress block, with little adaptation.

Figure 259 shows a heavy-weight garment intended to be worn like a jacket over another garment. This requires some adjustments (Figure 260).

Figure 259

Step 1

Lower the back and front necklines, and raise the shoulder-armhole point for shoulder pads, by the amounts shown. Lower and widen the armholes and allow more width across the back and chest. Also add more width at the side seams from the armhole to the hem line as shown.

The amount of adjustment varies according to the thickness of the garments expected to be worn underneath the jacket.

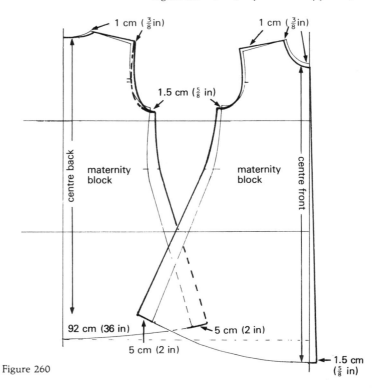

Figure 260

103

Step 2
Outline in black tape on a
pregnant figure, or on a
padded dress form, the
desired position of the
yoke and the length of the
smock or jacket (Figure
261). Measure the
distances from the centre
shoulder and from the pit
of the neck to the yoke
line and to the full length
(Figure 262). Transfer
these measurements to the
outlined maternity blocks
(Figure 263(a) and (b)).
Add a button stand of
2.5 cm (1 in) to the centre
front.

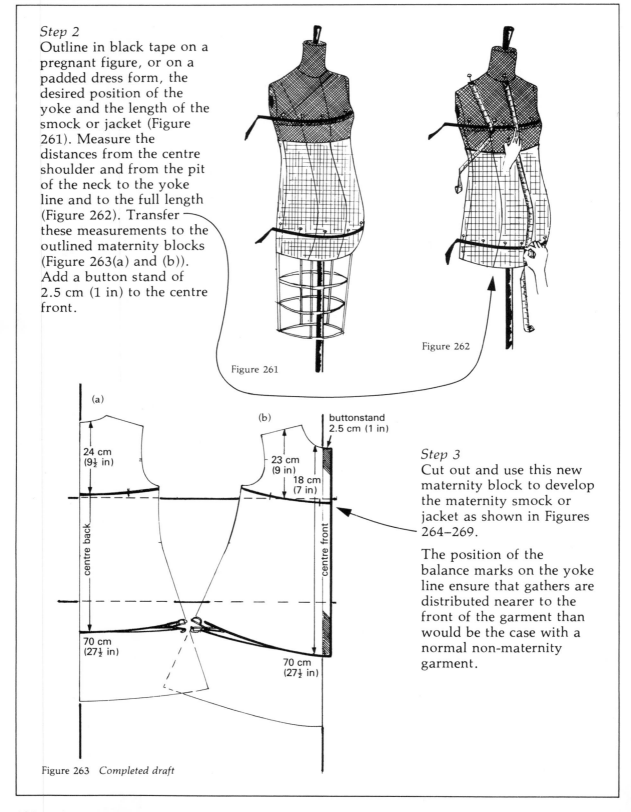

Figure 261

Figure 262

Step 3
Cut out and use this new
maternity block to develop
the maternity smock or
jacket as shown in Figures
264–269.

The position of the
balance marks on the yoke
line ensure that gathers are
distributed nearer to the
front of the garment than
would be the case with a
normal non-maternity
garment.

Figure 263   *Completed draft*

Developing the maternity smock or jacket

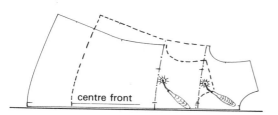

Figure 264

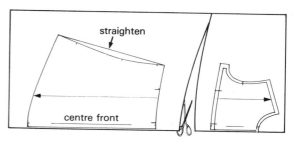

Figure 265

Step 1
Place the block on the horizontal line. Outline the yoke. Trace yoke line (Figure 264). Slide the pattern to the left on the horizontal line. Outline and trace the remaining part of the pattern. Cut out the yoke and other pattern piece (Figure 265).

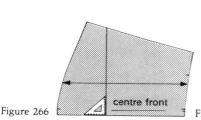

Figure 266

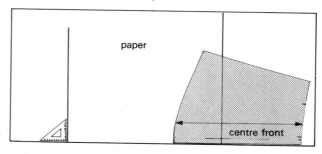

Figure 267

Step 2
On the pattern and on the paper draw a line at right angles to the centre front (Figure 266). Place the pattern on paper, matching the line on the pattern with the line on the paper (Figure 267).

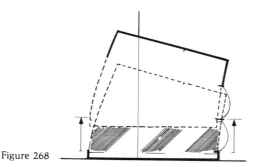

Figure 268

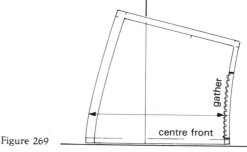

Figure 269

Step 3
Outline the pattern to the first balance mark. Crossmark. Also crossmark second gathering balance mark on the pattern paper *before* sliding the pattern forward to match the first balance mark on the pattern with the second crossmark on pattern paper (this doubles the gathering area). Outline the remaining side-section of the pattern including the crossmarking of the second balance mark. Complete the pattern as shown in Figure 269.

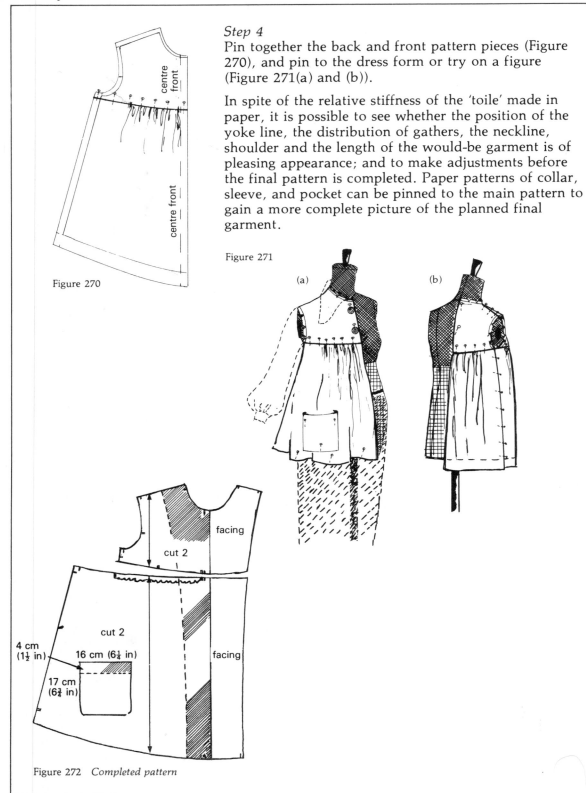

Figure 270

Step 4

Pin together the back and front pattern pieces (Figure 270), and pin to the dress form or try on a figure (Figure 271(a) and (b)).

In spite of the relative stiffness of the 'toile' made in paper, it is possible to see whether the position of the yoke line, the distribution of gathers, the neckline, shoulder and the length of the would-be garment is of pleasing appearance; and to make adjustments before the final pattern is completed. Paper patterns of collar, sleeve, and pocket can be pinned to the main pattern to gain a more complete picture of the planned final garment.

Figure 271

(a)

(b)

Figure 272 *Completed pattern*

Collars for maternity dresses

Collars are an important part of
garments. Whether a garment has a collar
or not may be related to its function,
such as protection during stormy
weather, or to underline a current vogue
or a new fashion trend.

The thoughtful designer will select a
suitable collar shape, a fabric and
possible trimmings to suit the wearer's
neck and to flatter her face.

Because collars are looked at more often
than any other garment feature it is well
worth developing a variety of well-fitting
collar patterns (Figure 273(a)–(i)). The
technique of modelling lends itself
favourably to this end: the shape of the
collar, its degree of roll, the position on
the neckline or the shoulders can be
noted immediately and if desired,
changed instantly. The small size of a
collar is an advantage to the process of
modelling and the speed with which it
can be carried out. (See also Chapter 7 of
Modelling and Flat Cutting for Fashion 1.)

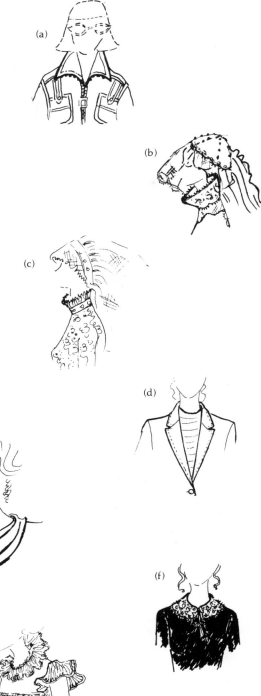

Figure 273

Soft jacket collar (Figure 274)

Figure 274

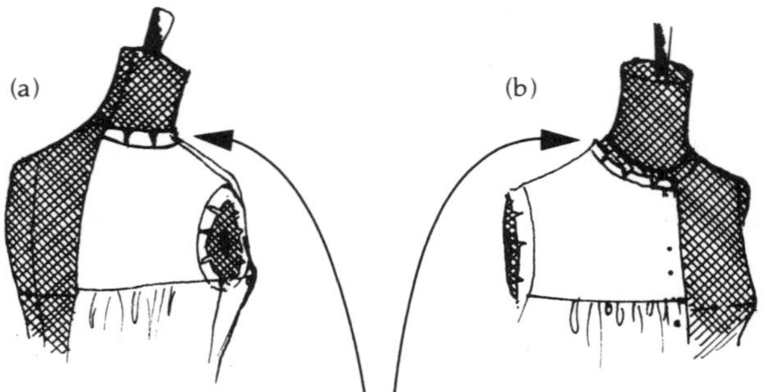

Figure 275

Step 1
Lower the neckline all around by 1 cm ($\frac{3}{8}$ in) (Figure 275(a) and (b)).

Step 2
To arrive at the measurements for cutting the modelling fabric, measure from the nape of the neck to an approximate position of the desired collar point (Figures 276 and 277). Add on 2 cm ($\frac{3}{4}$ in) to give a total of 35 cm (14 in) in length.

The width is obtained by measuring from the pit of the neck to an approximate position of the desired collar point, allowing for roll. Add on 2 cm ($\frac{3}{4}$ in) to give a total of 20 cm (8 in) in width (Figure 278).

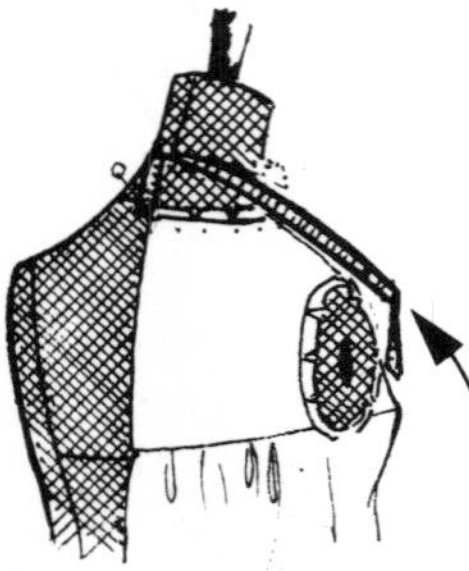

Figure 276

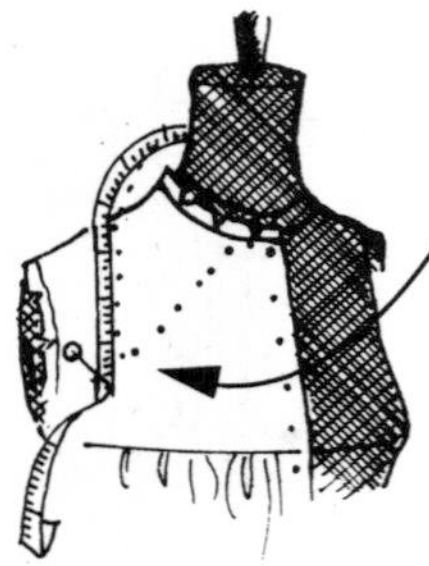

Figure 277

Figure 278

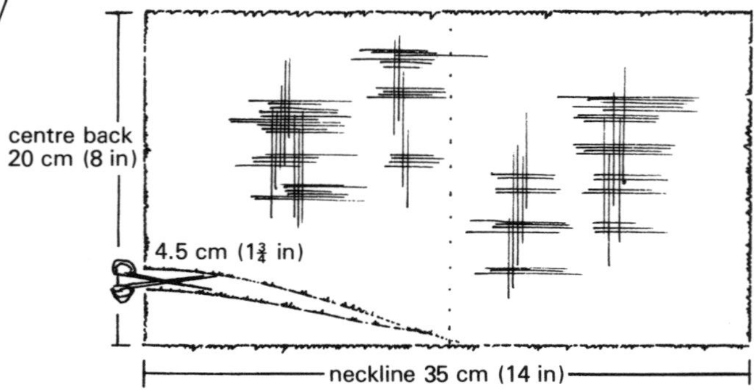

centre back 20 cm (8 in)

4.5 cm ($1\frac{3}{4}$ in)

neckline 35 cm (14 in)

Figure 279

Step 3
Cut a rectangle of modelling fabric such as calico. Mark the left short side *centre back*. The bottom long edge represents the *neckline*. On the centre back line from the neckline measure up 4.5 cm (1¾ in). Cut away a crescent-shaped piece of fabric to approximately half-way across the fabric (Figure 279).

Step 4
Pin the centre back edge of the modelling fabric to the centre back of garment neckline and dress form, arranging the bulk of the fabric above the neckline. Pin and snip as shown in Figure 280. Continue to the front, snipping the edge where required, and easing the fabric a little over the shoulder area. Fold the collar fabric down occasionally to ensure a good roll and to prevent any tightness. The centre back of the collar must remain in the centre back position and must not be pulled away from it (Figure 281).

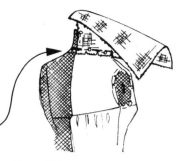

Figure 280

Figure 281

Step 5
Outline the shape of the collar in black tape. Cut the fabric on the crease line to centre front point (Figure 282). Continue outlining the collar stand and mark all pinned lines (Figure 283). Place balance marks at shoulder position (Figure 284). The completed pattern is shown in Figure 285.

Develop the top collar as for the jacket collar (Figure 31 on page 25).

Figure 282

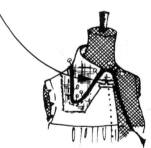

Figure 283

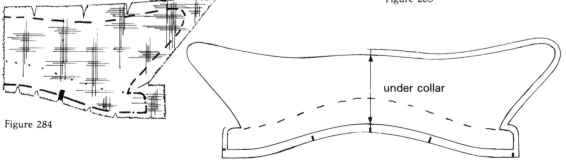

Figure 284

Figure 285   *Completed pattern*

under collar

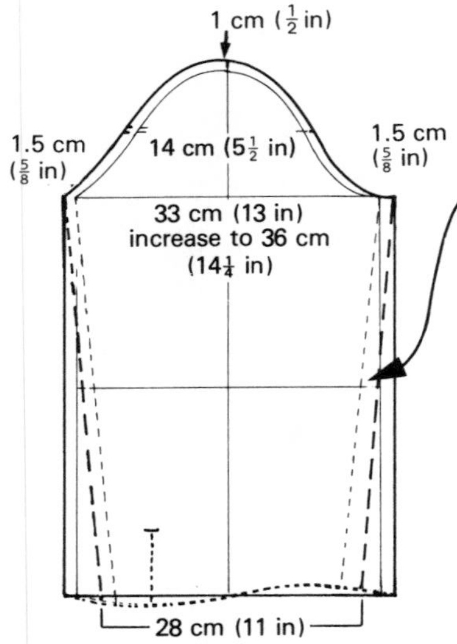

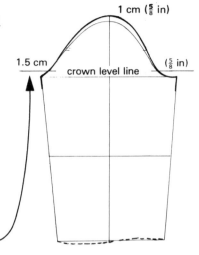

1 cm ($\frac{1}{2}$ in)

1.5 cm ($\frac{5}{8}$ in)

14 cm (5$\frac{1}{2}$ in)

1.5 cm ($\frac{5}{8}$ in)

33 cm (13 in)
increase to 36 cm
(14$\frac{1}{4}$ in)

28 cm (11 in)

Figure 286

Sleeves for the maternity jacket or smock

For the maternity smock (Figure 258) outline the *straight sleeve block* (page 13). For the jacket (Figure 259) outline the *fitted sleeve block* (page 12) in fine broken lines within the straight sleeve block diagram. Omit the wrist dart.

Step 1
Raise the sleeve crown and enlarge the sleeve circumference throughout as shown. See also Figure 34 for *two-piece sleeve* measurement chart.

1 cm ($\frac{5}{8}$ in)

1.5 cm

crown level line

($\frac{5}{8}$ in)

Step 2
Raise the sleeve crown a further 1 cm ($\frac{3}{8}$ in) if the jacket has shoulder pads. Draw two short horizontal lines 1.5 cm ($\frac{5}{8}$ in) above and parallel to the crown level line.

Figure 287

Step 3
Pivot the underarm points touching the horizontal lines (Figure 288), and outline. Add seam allowances and check for fit.

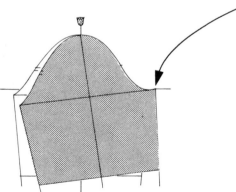

Figure 288

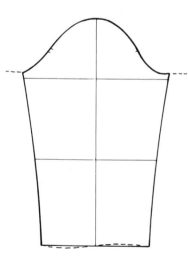

Figure 289 *Completed pattern*

Raglan style maternity smock (Figure 290)

Centralize the *basic maternity smock pattern* (Figure 260). (Instructions for centralizing the bodice and sleeve blocks are given in Chapter 7 of *Modelling and Flat Cutting for Fashion 2*.)

Step 1
Lower the armhole of the smock pattern but do not raise the shoulder as shown in Figure 260. Lower the neckline (Figure 291) by the amounts given, shorten the hem line and straighten side seams.

Step 2
Centralize and shorten the underarm seam of the straight sleeve (Figure 286) to 4 cm ($1\frac{3}{4}$ in).

The pattern is now ready for further development for the raglan style maternity smock (Figure 290).

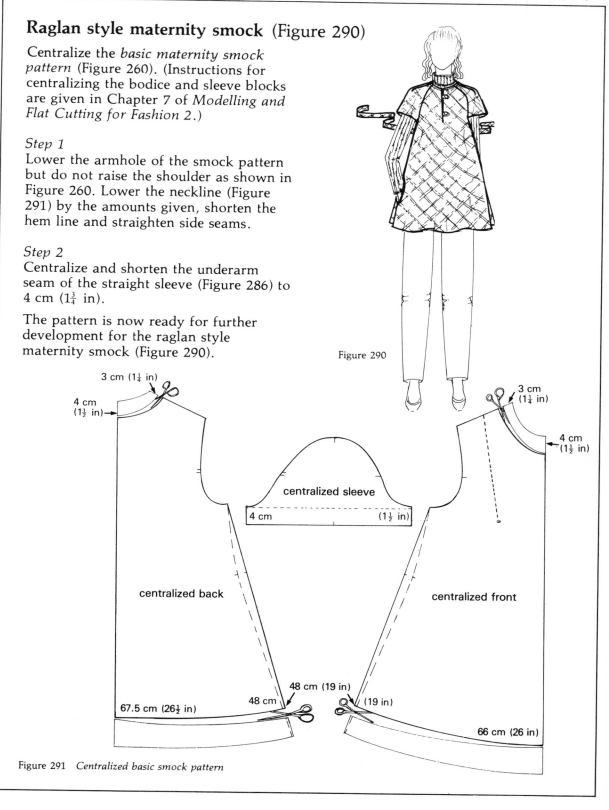

Figure 290

Figure 291   *Centralized basic smock pattern*

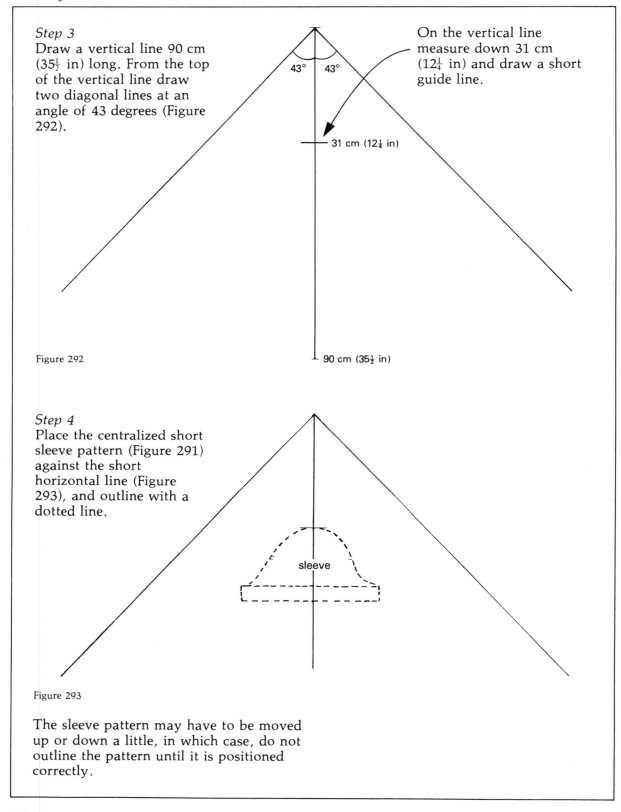

Step 3
Draw a vertical line 90 cm
(35½ in) long. From the top
of the vertical line draw
two diagonal lines at an
angle of 43 degrees (Figure
292).

43°   43°

On the vertical line
measure down 31 cm
(12¼ in) and draw a short
guide line.

31 cm (12¼ in)

Figure 292

90 cm (35½ in)

Step 4
Place the centralized short
sleeve pattern (Figure 291)
against the short
horizontal line (Figure
293), and outline with a
dotted line.

sleeve

Figure 293

The sleeve pattern may have to be moved
up or down a little, in which case, do not
outline the pattern until it is positioned
correctly.

Step 5
Place the centralized back
and front smock patterns
(Figure 291) to the left and
right diagonal lines. These
lines represent the centre
back and centre front of
the patterns.

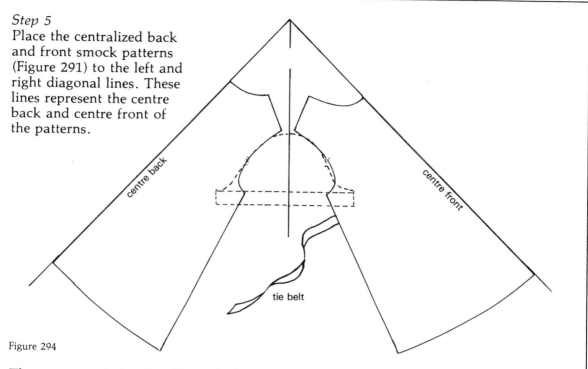

Figure 294

The upper armholes should touch the upper left and
right edge of the sleeve crown and armhole; sleeve
balance marks should align, or almost align, if possible.

Step 6
The shoulder-armhole points will be some way above
the short horizontal guide line and the distance between
the shoulder-neck points can vary between 6 and 11 cm
($2\frac{1}{2}$ and $4\frac{1}{2}$ in). The reason for this variance can be
traced to the difference in the shape of the armholes of
patterns which are in common use in industry, colleges
or commerce.

Step 7
Draw raglan style lines as shown in Figure 295, touching
back and front balance marks (or almost touching if this
creates better and more pleasing lines) and connect with
back and front lower armhole curves. Complete the
shoulder dart, which will be sewn as a seam, following
the natural curve of the shoulder as shown. The front
shoulder is 15 cm (6 in) and the back shoulder
measurement is 15.5 cm ($6\frac{1}{8}$ in). The sleeve illustrated in
Figure 298 shows more width at the hem level and
would have more ease of movement at the underarm
than this sleeve provides. Further development is
therefore required.   *(see overleaf)*

Step 8

Trace the sleeve from the draft and cut out. Outline on a new sheet (Figure 296).

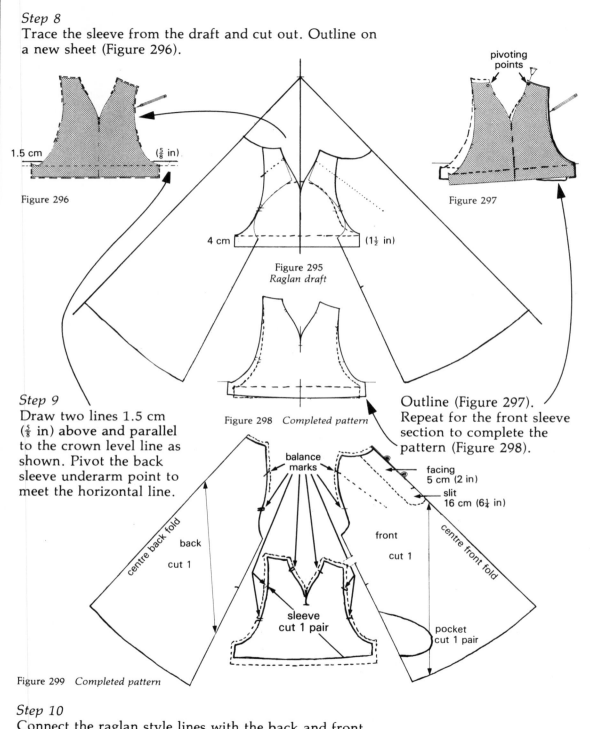

1.5 cm ($\frac{5}{8}$ in)

Figure 296

pivoting points

Figure 297

4 cm (1½ in)

Figure 295
Raglan draft

Figure 298   *Completed pattern*

Outline (Figure 297). Repeat for the front sleeve section to complete the pattern (Figure 298).

Step 9

Draw two lines 1.5 cm ($\frac{5}{8}$ in) above and parallel to the crown level line as shown. Pivot the back sleeve underarm point to meet the horizontal line.

balance marks

facing 5 cm (2 in)

slit 16 cm (6¼ in)

centre back fold

back cut 1

front cut 1

centre front fold

sleeve cut 1 pair

pocket cut 1 pair

Figure 299   *Completed pattern*

Step 10

Connect the raglan style lines with the back and front underarm points. Trace on to new paper. Draw grain lines and add seam turnings.

Waisted maternity garments

Waisted maternity garments, such as skirts and trousers, tend to cause constructional problems. This can be seen at once if one studies the contours of the pregnant figure. To begin with the position of the waist line is difficult to define. If a tape were tied around the waist it would come to rest on line 1 (Figure 300). Yet lines 2 and 3 look more like possible waist lines. Further, the developing abdominal circumference in itself presents difficulties. The skirt or trousers must allow for expansion throughout the best part of six months and should also be as flattering to the figure as possible. Designers have produced garments with deep folds, gathers and wrapovers, which can be let out (Figure 301). This is satisfactory but it also increases the circumference below the hip level when the garment is let out, and makes the wearer look large where she would dearly love to present a relatively trim fit.

The nicest looking skirts and trousers are those that are cut to allow for expansion in the abdominal region, and taper to normal measurements below the hip level. Such garments are loosely fitted in general, and the waist front is gathered by a slotted-through adjustable elastic band (Figure 302(a)). Other styles have insets of elasticized fabric (Figure 302(b)) or have the abdominal section simply cut out altogether with a buttonholed elastic band slotted through the liberally cut waist for adjustment as required (Figure 302(c)).

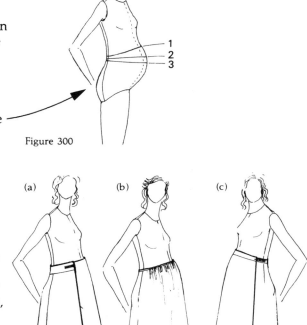

Figure 300

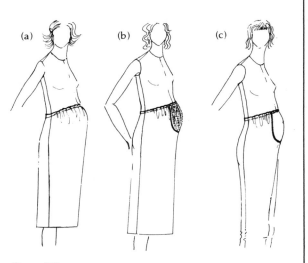

Figure 301   *(a) Deep folds; (b) gathers; (c) wrapover*

Figure 302

Maternity skirt with cascade drapery

Step 1

Cut out two pieces of mull, one to waist
level for the left side of the skirt and the
other to above waist level for the right
wrapover side of the skirt and drapery
(Figure 304). Pin mull representing the
left side to the padded maternity dress
form or pregnant figure, beginning at
centre back (Figure 305). Pin the other
piece of mull to the centre back seam,
wrap loosely over to the left side,
aligning centre front lines. Outline the
wrap and cut away all superfluous fabric
(Figure 306). Allow cascade drapery to
drop and pin two short pleats (Figure
307). The drapery may require further
reshaping to run gently in a curved line
into the hem line.

(a)   (b)

Figure 303

Step 2

Pin dart allowances as darts or, if
preferred, as side seams, continuing to
hem line, or elasticate with the waistband.

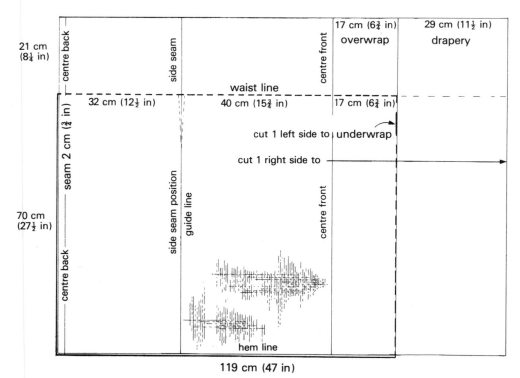

Figure 304

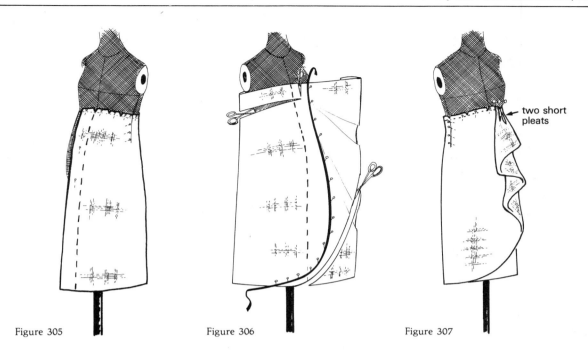

Figure 305   Figure 306   Figure 307

two short
pleats

Step 3

Mark the toile carefully. Remove from the dress form
and improve lines. Transfer to the pattern paper. Add
seam allowances. Fasten with Velcro.

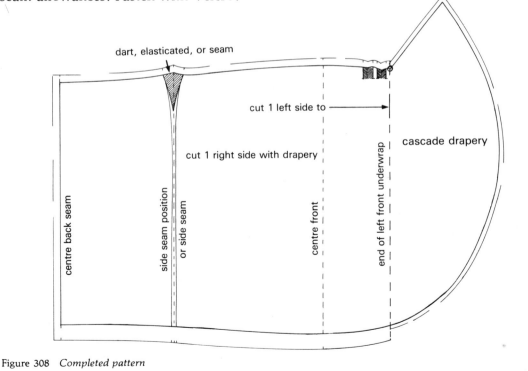

dart, elasticated, or seam

cut 1 left side to →

cut 1 right side with drapery

cascade drapery

centre back seam

side seam position
or side seam

centre front

end of left front underwrap

Figure 308   *Completed pattern*

Development of basic maternity skirt cut flat

All maternity patterns are developed from blocks one size larger than normal.

Step 1
Outline the *back* and *front skirt blocks* (page 12). Draw level P line 33 cm (13 in) below the waist line (Figure 310). All increases of measurement occur above the level P line.

Step 2
Square up from hem lines. This creates two rectangles, one representing the front, the other the back skirt pattern. Cut out in card. Mark pivoting point P on the front rectangle. Use these card rectangles to develop the maternity skirt (Figure 311).

Figure 309

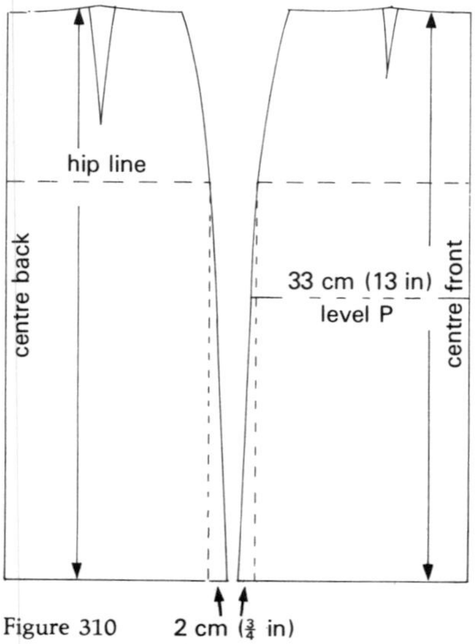

hip line

centre back

33 cm (13 in)
level P

centre front

Figure 310   2 cm (¾ in)

hip line

centre back

P
pivoting
point

centre front

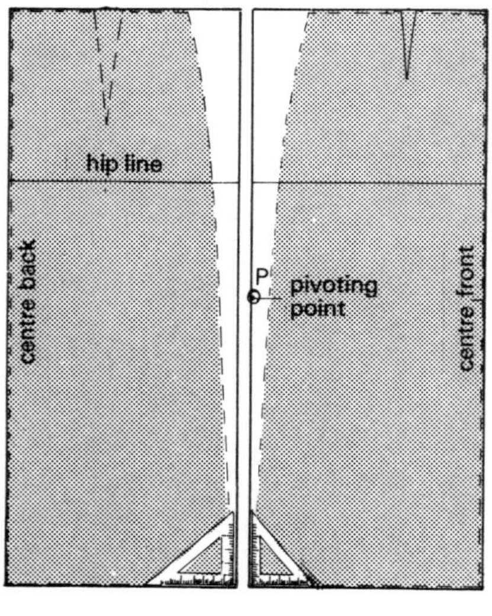

Figure 311

Step 3
Outline the front rectangle. Extend the waist line to the left (Figure 312).

Step 4
Pivot the card rectangle to the marked point and outline (Figure 313).

Step 5
The completed front pattern is shown in Figure 314 and is now ready for further development.

Step 6
Outline the back rectangle. Reduce the waist line at the side seam to pivoting point level by the same amount as that by which the front waist line was increased (2.5 cm (1 in)). Back and front side seam angles are now the same (Figure 316).

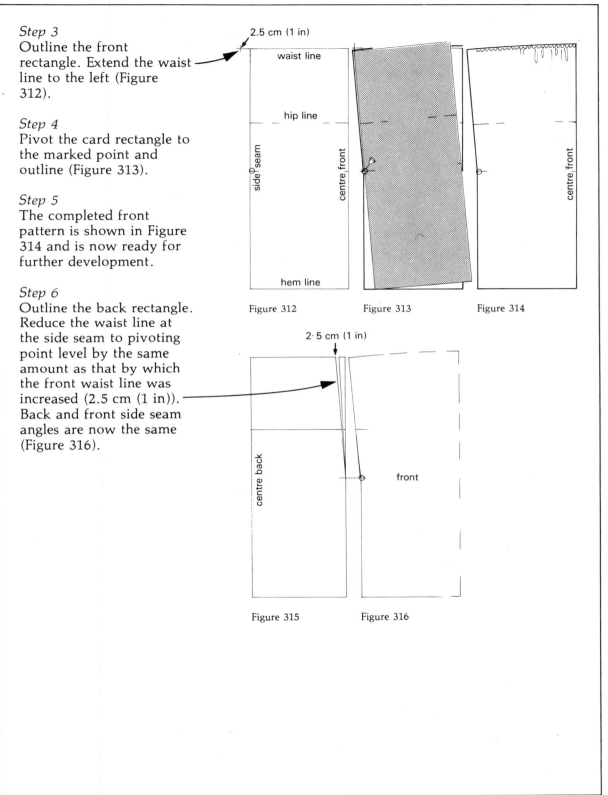

Figure 312   Figure 313   Figure 314

Figure 315   Figure 316

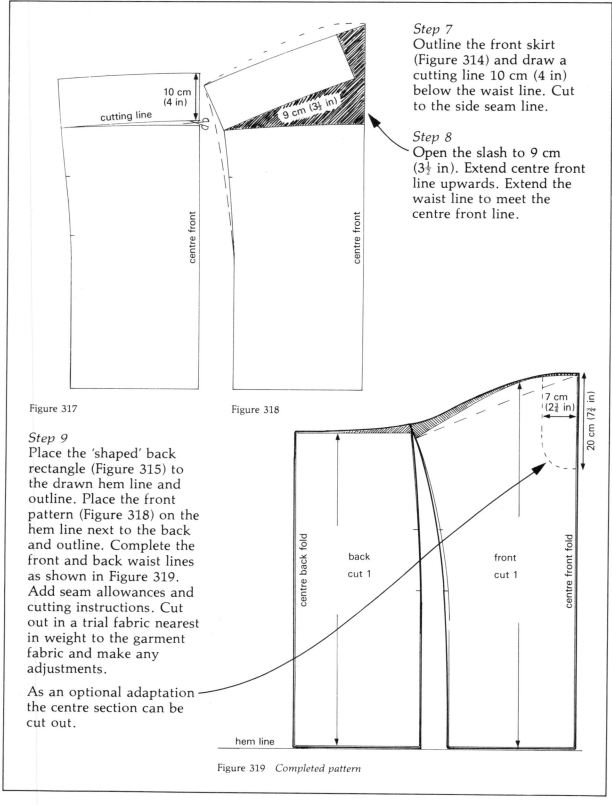

10 cm
(4 in)

cutting line

9 cm (3½ in)

centre front

centre front

Figure 317

Figure 318

Step 7
Outline the front skirt (Figure 314) and draw a cutting line 10 cm (4 in) below the waist line. Cut to the side seam line.

Step 8
Open the slash to 9 cm (3½ in). Extend centre front line upwards. Extend the waist line to meet the centre front line.

Step 9
Place the 'shaped' back rectangle (Figure 315) to the drawn hem line and outline. Place the front pattern (Figure 318) on the hem line next to the back and outline. Complete the front and back waist lines as shown in Figure 319. Add seam allowances and cutting instructions. Cut out in a trial fabric nearest in weight to the garment fabric and make any adjustments.

As an optional adaptation the centre section can be cut out.

7 cm
(2¾ in)

20 cm (7¾ in)

centre back fold

back
cut 1

front
cut 1

centre front fold

hem line

Figure 319 *Completed pattern*

Basic maternity trousers (Figure 320)

All maternity patterns are developed from blocks one size larger than normal.

Step 1

Outline the *standard width trousers pattern* (Figure 67) and superimpose the *upper part of the skirt development* (Figure 319) on to the trousers pattern.

Allow additional width where shown in Figure 321.

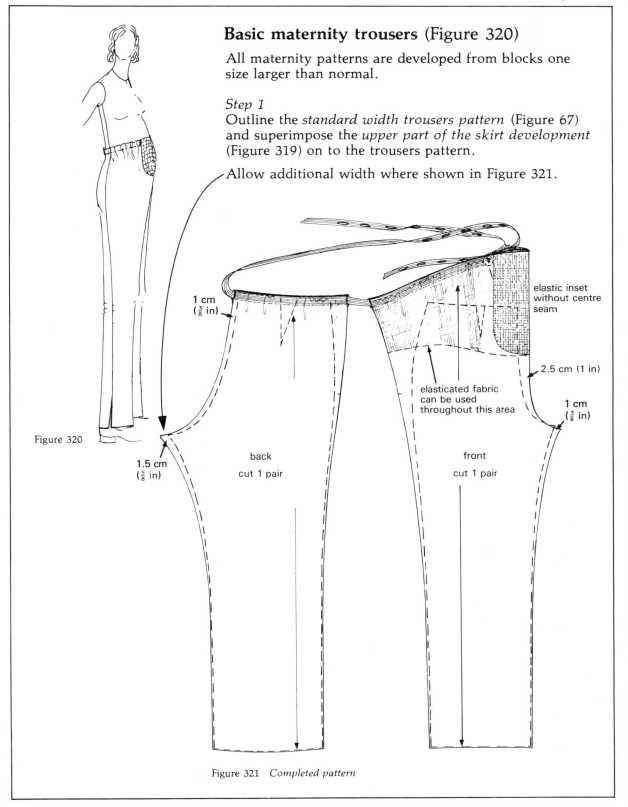

Figure 320

1 cm
(⅜ in)

1.5 cm
(⅝ in)

back
cut 1 pair

elastic inset
without centre
seam

2.5 cm (1 in)

elasticated fabric
can be used
throughout this area

1 cm
(⅜ in)

front
cut 1 pair

Figure 321 *Completed pattern*

Suppliers

Suppliers of pattern papers and card and cutting room equipment

E. Alexander & Co. (Int) Ltd., 656 Forest Road, London E17 3ED
and at Unit 9, Central Park Estate, Trafford Park, Manchester

S. Christy & Co., 60–62 Dublin Road, Belfast BT2 7HP

Cutting Room Supplies Ltd., 5 Newton Street, Piccadilly, Manchester M1 1HN

J. Davis (London) Ltd., 'Duro' House, Station Estate, Eastwood Close, London E18 1BY

Grancut Pattern Papers, Samuel Grant Ltd., Garnet Road, Leeds LS11 5LA

Morplan Garment Trade Supply Service, 56 Great Titchfield Street, London W1P 8DX
also at 50 Stroud Green Road, London N4

Morris & Ingram (London) Ltd., 17 Upper King Strett, Leicester

Wm. & A. M. Robb Ltd., 6 Dixon Street, Glasgow G1 4AS

Rudkin Brown Ltd., Chatham Street, Leicester

Charles Threlfall Ltd., Bridge Street, Linwood, Renfrewshire

B. S. & W. Whiteley Ltd., Pool Paper Mills, Pool-in-Wharfedale, Otley

Suppliers of calico and mull

Ascher (London), 299a Edgware Road, London W2

William Gee Ltd., 520 Kingsland Road, London E8

MacCulloch & Wallis Ltd., 25–26 Dering Street, London W1

Henry Mariot & Co. Ltd., Manchester

Siegel & Stockman Ltd., 301 Seddon House, Barbican, London EC2Y 8BX

Samuel Simpson & Co. Ltd., Manchester

Suppliers of dress forms

R. D. Franks Ltd., Kent House, Market Place, Oxford Circus, London W1N 8EJ

Kennett and Lindsell Limited, Crow Lane, Romford, Essex RM7 0ES

Siegel & Stockman Ltd., 301 Seddon House, Barbican, London EC2Y 8BX

Suppliers of *Modelling and Flat Cutting for Fashion 1–3* and other books on pattern cutting and fashion

W. & G. Foyle Ltd., 119 Charing Cross Road, London WC2

R. D. Franks Ltd., Kent House, Market Place, Oxford Circus, London W1N 8EJ

Hatchards Ltd., 187 Piccadilly, London W1

Morplan, 56 Great Titchfield Street, London W1P 8DX

A. R. Mowbray & Co. Ltd., 28 Margaret Street, London W1

W. H. Smith & Son Ltd., 10 New Fetter Lane, London EC4 and branches

Index